BLONDEST HOUR

BLONDEST HOUR

One Man's Heroic Fight to Save the Nation from a Killer Virus

Mark Husbands

V

VULPINE

PRESS

Published by Vulpine Press in the United Kingdom in 2025

Cover by Vulpine Press

ISBN: 978-1-83919-630-0

www.vulpine-press.com

To: Nita, Rekha and James

Second Edition

The first edition was left in the third cubicle along in the gentleman's rest room at the Nelson's Arms on the Old Kent Road. Despite the offering of a substantial reward for its return (£25.00) no information has been forthcoming.

Acknowledgements

The author gratefully acknowledges MI6, classified Whitehall documents and, frankly, snarky Downing Street sources, to whom he is forever indebted. The author is also unable to let the contribution of Eton and Oxford University pass unnoticed as without them none of the events in this book would be possible.

Pages Redacted at the Request of MI6

P32, P45, P67, P119 - 134: a list of the top 15 most useless baronesses in Britain; P219: schematic drawings of Mr Rees-Mogg's steam-powered wheelbarrow; and detailed maps of Mr Johnson's holiday movements, due to security concerns (P134-137).

AI Transparency

Alexa was used extensively to confirm dates, the size of Boris's bath towel, order the coffee, cross the t's, dot the i's and basically write the whole damn thing.

Introduction

A Brief History of British Epidemics

In the olden days, Britain was a world-beating nation when it came to infectious diseases. The first outbreak of measles (coincidentally the first disease to be spelt incorrectly as mezils) was followed by the black death in June 1548. After that, more creative diseases jumped on the bandwagon – plague, pestilence, French pox, gaol fever,[1] smallpox (slightly less garlicky and irritating than the previously mentioned pox) and influenza – the forerunner of the modern-day terminal illness known as The Influencer.

That anyone survived the ravages of these deadly epidemics was a testament to Britain's medical services. In those times, GP practices were desperately undermanned, due in no small part to the fact that they were run exclusively by witches (witchcraft being more effective than homeopathy). They were equipped with only the most rudimentary protective equipment – pointy hats, broomsticks, black cats and first aid kits containing such breakthrough medications (following phase II medical trials) as eye of newt and toe of frog.

---

[1] Known as Saturday Night Fever – USA

Staffing levels reached a tipping point when King James the First of England, previously known as King James the Sixth of Scotland, and before that, the king formerly known as Prince, decreed that all witches should be burned at the stake. This rash decision decimated the NHS at a stroke.

It should be noted that disease didn't end because the olden days stopped. Far from it. In the last 100 years or so, Britain has been invaded by:

- Spanish Flu (foreign import – possibly from Spain) – 1918 – 200,000 deaths
- Asian flu (foreign import – China) – 1957/8 – 33,000 deaths
- Hong Kong Flu (foreign import – China) – 1968 – 80,000 deaths
- Swine flu (foreign import – Mexico) – 2009 – 457 deaths

The main finding of the Black Death inquiry, which began in 1548 and ended in 2009,[2] recommended that the numbers seven, eight and nine should be banned. Like every other inquiry in the history of Britain, these findings were studiously ignored.

---

[2] A gap of almost 500 years – the average length of time for a British government inquiry

A Brand Spanking New Virus

By December 2019 things had gone a bit quiet on the pandemic front. The Chinese Communist Party decided that what the world needed, apart from shonky plastic goods, mobile telephony, forced labour and state-sponsored torture, was a brand, shiny new virus. So, they invented one in a town in the middle of nowhere called Wuhan, and it was an absolute zinger. The problem for the Chinese leadership was that they couldn't swerve blame for the virus onto the Spaniards because of social media. The Mexicans tried to claim responsibility early doors, but everyone realised they were only trying to make up for their previous feeble attempt at starting a pandemic.

The first case in China was confirmed in early December, and the cat was soon out the bag. After rampaging through a wet market and causing mayhem in hospitals, the new virus hatched a devious plan for a world tour and developed an effective region-based distribution strategy. The big question was, how would world leaders react?

Russia
Russian president and crazed basket case Vladimir Putin was pre-occupied with a lengthy to-do list:

- Update the Ministry of Poisoning (MOP) with some prospective new candidates.
- Amalgamate the Ministry of Falling off a Balcony (MOFB) with the Ministry of Falling out of Windows (MOFW) and ensure compliance with new health and safety regulations.
- Instruct Oleg, at the Ministry of Cavalcades (MOC), to stop taking the piss and order the presidential cavalcade to turn left out of the presidential villa gates on Tuesdays rather than right, thus avoiding the revolting sight of peasants eating shit in their fields and, more importantly, cutting the journey time to the gym by over three minutes.
- Arrange a Zoomski with senior members at the Ministry of Demonising Foreigners (MODF) to organise a daily Demonise Foreigners Day.
- Meet with the Ministry of Death Threats (MODT) heads of department to discuss changing the colour of death threat Post-its – Day-Glo yellow does not strike the right tone.
- Presentation to the Ministry of Tie Selection (MOTS) to radically overhaul the current sartorial options.

Current tie option:
MON – grey
TUE – grey/black stripe
WED – grey
THU – Black/grey stripe
FRI – grey

SAT – not required – bare-chested horse-riding day
SUN – not required – bare-chested karate day

Proposed tie option:
MON – grey
TUE – grey/black stripe
WED – grey/grey stripe
THU – Black/grey
FRI – navy
SAT – not required – bare-chested horse-riding day
SUN – not required – bare-chested karate day

Estimated time in a day left to deal with a virus (ETDLTDWV) –
nine minutes

China
The Chinese government was too busy locking up the people who
had locked up the people who had warned about a new virus, to
take any action to deal with the locked up people dying from the
new virus. Almost overnight, the ruling party smashed Chairman
Mao's long-standing record of throwing people into prison. The
state of panic reached the highest level since the record set by the
Pani-king dynasty in 1698.
ETDLTDWV – six minutes

USA
Popular American president Donald J. Trump had more than
enough on his plate in 2019. He was out every night draining

swamps, banning Muslims from being Muslims and extending the pay-as-you-go Botox contract for his wife, Melania, by another 12 months.

ETDLTDWV – three minutes

France

French president Macron had little, or no time left to deal with le virus following a violent reaction by les unions to his radical proposals for redesigning le croissant.

ETDLTDWV – seven minutes

Britain

The world was rapidly running out of leaders with the necessary time on their hands to deal with a new virus. Who would step up to the plate and save humanity from Armageddon? Bruce Willis was the obvious choice, but sadly, he was unavailable due to unforeseen circumstances.[3] The only candidate left standing, with plenty of spare time available, was the most significant political mind of the twenty-first century – Prime Minister of Great Britain and First Lord of the Zipwire – Boris Johnson.

Without a doubt, he had the right credentials, and his top ten lifetime achievements were the stuff of legend:

1. Won the Battle of Brexit by a country mile.
2. Set a new world record for smashing through a wall of polystyrene bricks in a JCB.

---

[3] Manual detonation of a nuclear bomb on an asteroid.

3. Gained a BETEC distinction for making model buses out of cardboard.
4. Single-handedly zip-wired the entire length of the Thames (in reverse).
5. Spent over £100m on virtual bridges, an aborted bridge to Ireland, assorted German water cannon, and dancing poles.
6. Stuck Belgian number plates on his car to avoid parking fines.
7. Quite reasonably hid in a dairy fridge as part of an impromptu Piers Morgan evasion manoeuvre.
8. Introduced the Boris Bike to the streets, council estates, and canals of London.
9. Stole a journalist's mobile phone
10. Hand built 40 new hospitals from scratch.

Small wonder then that many people worshipped him as the new messiah. This was despite the fact that the original messiah hadn't officially resigned and had a more 'on-trend' haircut.

Boris had far more pressing things on his mind when news of a new virus going ape leaked from Chinese social media whistleblowers. He was working 24/7 to finish packing away his collection of hand-curated sartorially challenged safari suits for a five-week holibob on the tropical paradise of Mustique. This was reportedly his ninety-ninth trip away since taking ministerial office, and he had high hopes of breaking through the one-hundred barrier by Christmas.

All was jolly kosher in the rarefied, toffish cloud of exuberance that enveloped Borisworld. He was enormously popular with the electorate after promising northerners a whizzy high-speed rail line to the summit of Mount Snowden, and for getting Brexit done, even though it was still very much at the half-baked stage.

Boris didn't ask to be the saviour of the entire world on his watch. He hadn't even planned on being prime minister beyond Brexit day. Cummings and the party grandees had recruited him to deliver Brexit and promised to let him go once it was done. Let's face it: being prime minister wasn't all it was cracked up to be, and the pay was barely above the minimum wage. Even his girlfriend, Young Symonds, said that the paper boy in Mummy and Daddy's village earned more than he did. The scene was now set.

This was his moment in history.

This was his chance to become the greatest prime minister in British history.

This was his BLONDEST HOUR.

December 2019

On a routine early morning patrol, Larry the Cat's finely tuned onboard sensors automatically switched to DEFCON two. He watched from the shadows as a large figure in a black balaclava and clutching a small dog padded down the stone steps barefoot, navigating with a thin beam of torchlight. The dog was gently lowered to the ground and carefully positioned in front of a motion sensor. The figure shuffled over to a pair of enormous steel catering-style refrigerators and opened the door.

The fridge light illuminated a pair of mad-staring eyes.

A hand snaked inside towards a bumper pack of forty-eight Cadburys Dairy Milk bars and carefully removed a handful. The thief leant against the fridge and removed the headgear.

It was Prime Minister of Britain and chocolate addict Boris Johnson.

Sweat dripped from his furrowed brow. He tore the wrapper off and wolfed down an entire bar in two bites. This was his medication, his sedative, his antidote to the raging helter-skelter stresses of high office. He attacked bar number two and gazed lovingly at the exposed chunks. If he could inject raw chocolate into his bloodstream, he would. After all, if he'd gone another thirty seconds without his fix, he'd have lost his mind. Dilyn, a poor man's Jack Russell, yelped.

'Stand your ground, man,' Boris hissed, throwing the dismal hound a small chunk to keep him quiet.

Dysfunction of an erectile nature was playing havoc with Boris's sex life these days, and Young Symonds insisted his weight needed to come down as it was hardly helping matters. She imposed strict rationing conditions: two chunks a day at weekends only. It was intolerable. He needed to shed untold amounts of poundage from the wibbly prime ministerial waistline. Short, ten-yard bursts of jogging in his fish patterned running shorts from behind some strategically placed shrubbery might fool a gullible press pack, but not Young Symonds. She was the senior forensic entomologist of *CSI: Downing Street*. Halfway through bar four, he rummaged in his dressing gown pocket and retrieved a crumpled-up sheet of paper. It was a top-secret map of a top-secret beach. Young Symonds had told him to memorise it for their upcoming five-week holibob, then destroy the evidence. The trouble with detail is that it was, on the whole, an unpalatable inconvenience for Boris.

The idea was to give the security chappies the slip and give themselves free rein to comfortably chill out by themselves. It was a top-notch plan, thought Boris. This is what the geometry of being a prime minister was all about:

- Thirty minutes of 'work' a day – tops.
- Dairy Milks and Pimms on tap

- Five-week luxury holidays in Elysian paradises, at the drop of a hat and all with the blessings of a grateful nation that would soon bask in the untold riches, freedoms, and fruit, in general, of Brexit.

There was one factor concerning his Dairy Milk heist that Boris hadn't considered.

Larry the Cat.

Larry was Downing Street's resident mouser and Honorary Protector of the Pantry, a position held by cats since the Middle Ages. Larry was intensely territorial, and the sight of a large human and a pathetic dog helping themselves to the fridge contents triggered all kinds of violent, psychopathic tendencies.

He rocketed across the pantry floor and leapt up onto a worktop. Before Boris had time to react, Larry had slashed his hand and snatched the half-eaten Dairy Milk out of his fingers. He shot off with Boris roaring at his heels like a psychopathic walrus. Out of sheer desperation, the prime minister attempted to execute the only sporting manoeuvre he knew. This was the trademark Johnson rugby tackle, known to be highly effective against repulsive ten-year-old children. Boris hurled himself at Larry, completely mistimed his lunge and clattered unceremoniously into a recycling bin overflowing with food scraps. Dilyn deserted his post, trotted over to his master and sniffed at the rasher of bacon attached to the Big White Chief's head. Thanks to Dilyn, the motion detector activated. Alarms shrieked. Sirens erupted. In seconds, the pantry door was blown off its hinges, and members of the security detail rushed down the steps, closely followed by Young Symonds. Larry fled back into the shadows.

'Boris, for God's sake,' she said as a security man helped the PM to his feet.

'Somnambulance, darling.'

'What happened to your hand?'

'Larry went berserk and tried to assassinate me.'

'So, you were sleepwalking, wandered into the pantry, and Larry attacked you for no good reason.'

'That's about the size of it, yes, Sweetpea.'

Young Symonds was unconvinced.

'Search him,' she barked to a security officer.

Two men went through the prime minister's pockets. The evidence was incriminating, to say the least:

EXHIBIT A: Four crumpled Diary Milk wrappers.

EXHIBIT B: One Dairy Milk bar – three chunks AWOL.

EXHIBIT C: One half-eaten Dairy Milk bar – two chunks remaining.

EXHIBIT D: Four fully intact Dairy Milk bars.

Young Symonds was incensed. She glared at her infinitely worse half (IWH) and Dairy Milk junkie. She scooped up Dilyn, span in a suitably incensed manner on her heels, and marched up the steps.

Larry watched the king of blather climb to his feet and shuffle morosely after Young Symonds. He was worried. Although he'd done his job and protected the pantry in full accordance with his constitutional obligations, a pissed-off Boris remained a pissed-off Boris at the end of the day. Something dangerous and unpredictable. After all, he had no problem with turning accepted conventions inside out. Look at that obscure prorogation stuff with Her Madge.

Now he saw it – a crumpled sheet of paper on the floor.

Boris had dropped it in the heat of battle. Larry padded towards it cautiously. *Hmmm…curious and curiouser.*

A Short Time Later
Prime Minister's Flat, Downing Street

It was a grey, baleful, wet morning. London found itself infected with a steady yet relentless drizzle – precisely what the city was designed for.

Weather like this helped to make the empire what it is today. The only way to escape both it and the dead-end job was to take immediate and evasive action by Fucking off Abroad (FOA). Englishmen for countless generations have been doing that in their droves. It's the reason they took ships to Africa and India, where conquering, pillaging, and enslaving readily embedded themselves into the British psyche, becoming known as colonial therapy. Two or three hundred years later, it rebounded back in their faces when they had their statues toppled by people with facial piercings, weird bras, and brandishing misspelt cardboard protest signs.

Ask any historian about The British Empire, and they'll tell you it was built on the principle of FOA and maybe also a smidgen of racist exploitation for financial gain.

Old Etonian and Prime Minister Boris Johnson felt as miserable and dank as the teeming drizzle. It was, without a doubt, conspiring against him, like a catastrophic relationship that deserved to be dragged to the vets, euthanised, and a donation made to the Woodland Trust. He stared wistfully out of his grimy study window while Lady Hortense, his nanny and part-time receptionist, bandaged the vicious claw scratches on his Dairy Milk scoffing hand.

He'd started packing three weeks ago for the Mustique holibob. That was a short time after giving Young Symonds a PowerPoint presentation on the subject of urgently needing to FOA in the grand tradition of the British aristocracy.

'He'll have to go,' he shouted as Lady Hortense stuck down a Band-Aid with ruthless efficiency. 'I want him out by close of play today.'

Young Symonds looked up from the in-depth glossy expanses of *Tatler*.

'Who has to go, Bumble? Dead Eye Raab? I'm not surprised,' she said. 'I did hear rumours that he'd once escaped from a psychiatric facility. The poor man belongs in a Nicholas Cage film.'

'No, not Dead Eyes, I meant the bloody cat.'

'Larry? Perhaps you provoked him. You do have an unerring knack for that sort of thing.'

As always, he resented her unerring knack for getting to the heart of his unerring knack.

'Nonsense, I went downstairs for one of my one hundred per cent hand-crafted organic, vegan-friendly, gluten-free, free-range energy bars when that bloody cat decided to assassinate me.'

Young Symonds eyed him doubtfully. 'Then why is there a dollop of chocolate decomposing in your hair?' she asked, with an equal dollop of scepticism twinkling in her eyes.

'It must have been planted there by that flea-ridden moggy.'

Young Symonds took a deep breath.

'You're lying through your teeth, Bumble, darling. You told me you were sleepwalking when we caught you. I know you too well. I think it's time this absurd habit of compulsive bullshitting stopped.' She picked the chocolate out of his hair. 'You need to grow up and start being more considerate to other people as well as cats. All this throw him out business is nothing but wounded pride.'

'I know, Sweetpea,' he said with a faint trace of a smirk.

'No, you don't know. This ghastly Boris first policy you've had for many years must be ditched. You need to take responsibility for your actions. We also made a pact. Dairy Milk is for weekends only and no more than two chunks.

The smirk vanished.

'Larry is officially a national treasure, young Master Boris, protected under the terms of the constitution since the thirteenth century,' huffed Lady Hortense.

'This is the problem with this country. The place is trapped in a Shakesperian tragedy – too many rules and regulations. We need to rip them up, take back control, return to high-quality politics, and unleash the UK's untapped potential,' Boris boomed, a trifle over-boomingly.

'Even a prime minister can't rip up the Magna Carta. There is a rule of law, Young Master Boris.'

Young Master Boris glowered at Lady Hortense and brandished his mobile phone. He punched some buttons.

'Marty, I need to know Pronto Tonto what the Magna Carta says about cats and biff-boffingly sharpish,' he said, feeling an immediate uptick in mood.

Within minutes, Martin Reynolds, Boris's Personal Private Secretary wallah, stood in the middle of the room clutching one of the original copies of the *Magna Carta.*

'So, where we stand on the thorny question of a prime minister being able to boot out Downing Street's resident *cattus horribilis*?' said Boris.

Martin flipped through the ancient parchment sheets.

'Here we are, sir. Page seventeen.' He tapped the page. 'The document clearly states that a cat, as resident mouser and stout protector of the pantry, cannot be exiled, executed or deprived of his tenancy unless he murders one of the king's cup-bearers.'

Boris squinted. 'Cup-bearers, Marty?'

'An officer of high rank who pours drinks for the ruling monarch and protects them from being poisoned by tasting them himself.'

'It sounds utterly ghastly.'

'Very likely, sir.'

'Thank you, Marty. Most enlightening.'

Marty turned on his heels and took England's constitution with him. Boris seemed deflated. He was powerless to kick out that bloody cat. It was like dealing with tedious Whitehall civil servants. He'd have to bide his time and resort to some biff-boffingly cunning subterfuge.

For Young Symonds, defending a small animal was more important than protecting the rights of a chocolate-addicted prime minister. She watched him waddling off to the bathroom. He'd been through a lot since becoming the new Messiah. Being worshipped 24/7 had taken its toll. FOA for five weeks was exactly what the dear boy needed to keep his flagging spirits up until Brexit Day, and he could safely resign before the madness descended.

Slightly Later
Downing Street Front Room

Larry the cat sat on the headrest of an antique chaise longue. He thought long and hard about his altercation with big rabid dog Boris last night. At least Mrs May wasn't in the habit of attempting to rugby tackle him. She and her husband, Sir Philip, who Donald Trump mistook for Woody Allen, the famous Hollywood director, treated him with a degree of respect and a carefully judged tasty morsel. Back in the good old days, he could sneak into the flat while she was updating her vast collection of 3.5-inch floppy discs. Licking the lint from out her crooked toes was, he felt, a small price to ensure his continued comfort, and he saw it as his duty, as a cat of the realm, to perform these kinds of heroic and selfless feats of endurance.

The Boris episode had left him decidedly skittish. In the short time he'd known the chief, one thing was for certain: the PM was a man who harboured a grudge and thwarting his chocolate heist was going to be right up there. The only way a cat could deal with this, his counsellor once told him after a particularly gruelling session, was to listen to his inner music. The problem with this pearl of psychiatric wisdom was that his inner music happened to be Metallica.

Being attacked by a pantry-raiding chocolate junkie had created a massive disturbance in the cat force. It was an absolute disgrace. Not only that, but the bozo-in-chief had dragged that well-known pestilential fuck-wit Dilyn along with him. Larry had big plans for the mutt and had developed a cunning dog-removal scheme. This mostly consisted of leaving the front door open and enticing the imbecilic hound into the great outdoors. The major flaw in his meticulously executed plan was that the epic little shit suffered from acute Stockholm syndrome. The last time he'd tried it, the moronic canine stood there shivering for half an hour until a panic-stricken Young Symonds came to his rescue.

Larry's focus on his patented Dilyn disposal scheme was broken by the sight of a tall man arriving outside the window and padlocking his bicycle to the number ten railings with an unfeasible amount of anti-theft devices. Through a rapidly shifting fog of anti-Dilyn thoughts, Larry watched Isambard Henry Beamish shake the rain off his clothing and march up to the front door. Beamish was a senior man in MI6 and, furthermore, a man who did not officially exist. He'd begun to show up every week ostensibly to brief the PM on intelligence matters, but to Larry's mind the visits were designed to keep tabs on Boris.

The doorbell rang. Pre-Young Symonds, the ringtone was far more befitting of high, if not outright dull, office, such as a marching band or the Eton boating song – a notoriously discordant favourite of every Tory PM since Pitt the Tone-Deaf. If the mood at number ten was particularly sombre, say after a major ministerial gaffe or the death of a generous party donor, the default setting was the tiresome dirge commonly known as the national anthem. Finding all this completely intolerable, old-fashioned and 'like, so cobwebby', Young Symonds had switched things up to something more contemporary. Today, it was something by the folk-rock maestros Mumford and Sons. Their music was over-accessorised with highly annoying accordions, banjos, and a bloody Flugelhorn – the musical equivalent of a cerebral aneurysm. What kind of monumental eejit would ever consider a flugelhorn as being intrinsic to any form of music? Larry found it completely baffling. He retrieved the map with his mouth from the chaise and, to a dreadful cacophony of appalling instruments, trotted out of the room.

Downing Street Entrance Hall

Larry had a soft spot for Beamish. There was something impressive about a human male who always wore a tux and was happy indulging a cat with some chin-scratching action.

'Good to see you, Larry. You're looking well,' said Beamish in his silky baritone.

Larry purred in delight. He allowed Beamish to take the folded-up secret map from his mouth.

'Is this for me? What a clever chap you are.' He placed the map inside a tux pocket and winked conspiratorially. Beamish's weekly intelligence briefing visits had become a necessity due to Boris's highly successful stint as foreign secretary. It hadn't taken long for the new messiah's inbuilt faux pas mechanism to kick in. He blazed a trail for professional foot-in-mouth gaffe-shitters everywhere, including:

- Making jokes about dead bodies in Libya.
- Reciting Kipling in Myanmar.
- Keeping Nazanin Zaghari Ratcliffe, a project co-ordinator in charge of grant applications, safely behind bars in an Iranian jail by saying she was there to train journalists. The Iranians, being Iranians and somewhat to the right of Vlad the Impaler, felt they had no choice but to keep her in prison for another twenty years. However, they generously agreed to only hang her upside down at weekends.

To the security services, this was a red flag nailed to the top of an old telephone box. It meant that the Big White Chief couldn't be trusted. He needed regular monitoring, and that's where Beamish came in.

Beamish headed through the hallway to the formidable new reception desk occupied by an equally formidable receptionist. Lady Hortense was a woman rumoured to have single-handedly repelled a Taliban attack in Helmand Province. She stood bolt upright in front of a fine example of Young Symonds' taste in fine art. These eclectic tastes ranged from assorted Banksy's to that one of the lady tennis player scratching her bum. All were guaranteed to discombobulate the most hardened headbanging backbencher. Beamish made a mental note that one of the Banksy's featured an inebriated Churchill smoking a joint and injecting himself in the arm with a syringe. Lady Hortense scrutinised MI6's finest over her horn-rimmed spectacles.

'You need to ring the bell,' she intoned, in a commanding yet strident voice that had once sent hardened jihadists running for the hills.

Beamish dutifully rang the bell, and she sprang into action – a minor adjustment of her horn-rimmed spectacles followed by a haughty sip of black tea.

'May I help you?' she asked with a searing note of mild disdain.

'It's me, Lady Hortense.'

She stared at him blankly, as if he'd wandered into Downing Street under the influence of the finest quality Mexicana magic mushrooms.

'I'm here to see the PM.'

'They all say that. Do you have an appointment?'

'I'm Beamish from MI6. MI6 does not make appointments, and I've been coming here every week since the PM moved into Downing Street.'

'Then you'll need to fill in a form,' she replied in impeccable cut-glass officialese and handed him a clipboard and a biro.

'MI6 does not fill in forms. It's a matter of national security. I need to see the PM.'

'That's what Mr Palchuk said.'

'Mr Palchuk?'

'The Latvian cultural attaché. He's been in waiting room four ever since.'

'This is extremely urgent.'

'Form,' barked Lady Hortense, tapping the clipboard with her standard issue pen.

'It never used to be like this.'

'Form filling in triplicate is only one of many improvements Mr Cummings has made to the place. He wants to grow this area of the organisation to achieve satisfactory outcomes, apparently. According to him, now we're out of Europe, we can make up our own rules.'

'Where would we be without bureaucracy?' pondered Beamish.

'Where indeed?' agreed Lady Hortense. Beamish filled out his form, and she dutifully filed it on a large tray labelled 'Forms'. She gestured towards waiting room #3.

'Mr Cummings personally vets all visitors. Please take a seat.'

Beamish ambled off to the waiting room, closely followed by Larry.

Downing Street Waiting Room #3

Beamish had no choice. He had to cool his heels for ten minutes before the door creaked open. A slovenly dressed man in an Ed Sheeran T-shirt and woollen beanie hat made an incongruous entrance. Far more special than just a common or garden 'adviser' or even a senior special adviser, Dominic 'Svengali' Cummings was the prime minister's trusted chief senior special adviser and, therefore, a God amongst men. Boris was under the delusional belief that he'd hand-picked him to coordinate and dream up a string of zap-pow slogans for his successful leave Brexit campaign, then paint them on the side of a bus. In truth, Cummings and the party grandees had recruited Boris purely for Brexit-specific reasons.

Cummings introduced himself and clicked his fingers. Immediately, a crack team of flunkeys rushed into the room and hastily rearranged all the chairs. To the casual observer, the previous arrangements looked perfectly acceptable. Cummings, however, was a stickler for detail. He was driven by an obsession with moving furniture according to ancient feng shui principles. His thought processes could only achieve peak thought when the energy levels of a room were correctly aligned. He indicated a chair for Beamish, and the underlings vanished as quickly as they came. Cummings fine-tuned their work using a satellite-linked laser protractor. Only when he was thoroughly satisfied did he take the chair directly opposite Beamish.

'I hear you want to see the chief,' said Cummings. His eyes betrayed a mild amusement carefully seasoned with a pinch of high-octane loathing.

'I have vital intelligence – strictly for the PM's ears only,' replied Beamish, remembering that his training had been most precise about not trusting a man with an unshaven chin or going about the place barefoot.

'You can tell me. I'm the Chief's chief senior special adviser,' countered Cummings, marshalling all the attitude his bone-splintering superego would allow.

'That's not protocol, I'm afraid, old chap.'

Cummings practically imploded. 'Protocol? I bloody well invented protocol.'

'You don't have MI6 clearance,' replied Beamish, narrowing his eyes and hoping against hope this dreadful man was joking.

'I practically am the PM. Who do you think makes all the decisions around here?'

'It doesn't work like that.'

'The PM will take a dim view of this. He's packing for a well-earned holiday in Mustique and doesn't want to be bothered by anything to do with anything.'

Beamish considered this for a moment. The man was even more deranged and delusional than the analysis in dossier DS/DC/697/a suggested. The unshaven chin explained a lot, perhaps even more so than the beanie hat, which appeared to be on the verge of spontaneously combusting.

'It's hardly democratic, if I were to brief an unelected representative of Her Madge's government,' said Beamish.

Cummings sat back. A rogue vein twitched on his forehead. He made a contemplative steeple with the fingers of both hands.

'I am the de facto PM when the PM is otherwise engaged in non-de facto affairs of state involving his de facto travel arrangements,' said Cummings. He leaned forward and waved his hands, doing his level best to get under Beamish's skin.

'I'm sorry, Mr Cummings. No can do.'

Cummings' brain clicked into full-on scheming overdrive.

'So how do I know you are who you say you are? What proof do I have that you are an MI6 operative?' demanded Cummings, jabbing an accusatory finger.

'Like all previous chief senior special advisers and prime ministers, you must go with the flow and assume I am who I say I am.

You know I've been coming here every week for the last few months. The PM is the only individual I'm at liberty to share intelligence with.'

'But Boris is more like a CEO. He delegates.'

'Then I need to see the CEO,' said Beamish, checking his watch. This caught Cummings' eagle eye.

'If you are MI6, that must be a special watch.'

'Special?'

'Yes, you know, chock full of gadgets. I bet it fires bullets, undoes ladies' underwear and remote starts your bombproof BMW. I take it you have an exploding pen?'

'I rather think you're confusing me with someone else.'

'I'm guessing you came here by gyrocopter?'

'No, thanks to austerity measures, I cycled here from Whitehall.'

'Let me see your watch, and you can see the PM.'

Reluctantly, Beamish slid the watch off his wrist. 'Don't, whatever you do, press the two side buttons simultaneously,' he warned.

This was a red flag to a bloodthirsty know-all of Cummings' calibre. Naturally, he pressed both buttons. The results were simultaneously instantaneous – a small harpoon blasted out on the end of a high-tensile steel wire. In the blink of an eye, it wrapped itself around the ceiling fan and yanked the hapless chief senior special adviser off his feet. It left him rotating quickly in a Tom Cruise, *Mission Impossible* laser maze position. Beamish admired his handiwork.

'That will give the spin doctors something to think about,' he quipped to Larry and raised his left eyebrow. Larry mewed in appreciation and hissed at Cummings.

'Larry, could you give me a hand here? I need to bypass security and get upstairs to see the Chief,' said Beamish.

Larry leapt up at a bronze bust of a young Winston Churchill on the mantelpiece that, for some reason, had a leopard print thong wrapped around its neck. A secret panel opened in the bookcase. Beamish slipped through and disappeared into the labyrinthine passages that lurked behind the Downing Street walls.

Downing Street Flat Bathroom

For prime minister, war hero, statesman and fifth greatest Briton of all time (after Churchill, Thatcher, Nelson, and Paddington the Bear), Boris Johnson, the day hadn't kicked off with a rip-roaring start. Unless you consider being savaged by a feral cat, deprived of your daily fix of Dairy Milk, and bollocked by your girlfriend to within an inch of your life as just peachy.

Matters had taken a slightly upward turn the moment he'd immersed himself in the jacuzzi[4] in his 'bath ready' Union Jack Speedos. There, he had time to think and re-enact a splendid British naval battle with a glass of champers on the go. In this case, it involved attacking the German World War Two battleship *Bismarck* using a fleet of British model warships, small aeroplanes, and three dinosaurs pilfered from Jacob Rees-Mogg's extensive

---

[4] Complete with patented hydromassage, a moulded in ice-ice bucket and red, white and blue LEDs.

Jurassic Park collection. Caught up in the heat of battle and bellowing a series of conflicting orders, he scarcely noticed part of the tiled wall opening and Beamish emerging into his bathroom from the starboard side.

'Morning, sir.'

'Beamish. WTAF!' exclaimed Boris.

'I'm sorry to barge in, sir; it's a matter of national security.'

'National security? More like national ruffle my feathers, I'm bound to say. Why didn't you ring the bloody bell?"

'I did, sir, and now I fear I'm scarred for life.'

'Flugelhorns?'

'Sadly, yes. I also had to fill in forms and survive interrogation by Mr Cummings.'

'Ah yes, Cummings. I fear the power has gone to his head.'

'I'm very sorry, sir.'

'Never apologise, Beamish. Not under any circumstances. It's been the family motto since the fifth Baronet Johnson ballsed up the Charge of the Light Brigade.'

'Indeed, sir.'

'Well, jolly well go and engage in some chatterage with Young Symonds while I finish torpedoing Fritz. I'll be with you in a squiff of a jiff. I believe you know her?'

'We are acquainted, yes, sir.'

'While you're about it, do me a favour and ask Lady Hortense to pronto up my bathrobe.'

Downing Street Flat Lounge

Minutes later, Beamish sipped a glass of chilled Prossey while Young Symonds hoovered around what she'd been led to believe was a rare nineteenth-century silver dancing pole.

'You can't come marching in here at the drop of a hat, Beamy,' she chided.

'No choice, I'm afraid, ma'am. If there is a matter of national security, I'm duty-bound to tell the chief. Operational parameters and all that.'

'It's incredibly inconvenient. Boris is highly unstable when co-ordinating the fleet and still hasn't finished his packing. Do you have any idea how many safari suits one man needs?'

'One can only imagine, ma'am.'

At this, the bathroom door practically flew off its hinges. The Prime Minister and Third Lord of the Wide-Open Bathrobe, stomped into the middle of the room in a pungent cloud of aromatic essential oils. Lady Hortense bustled around him with a large towel.[5]

'A young man should be tackle in, not tackle out at all times, Young Master Boris.'

'Yes, of course, nanny, it won't happen again.'

He placed two dripping model warships on the mantelpiece.

'Well, that puts paid to the Bismarck.' He took his eyes off the ships and turned his attention to Beamish. 'I'll repeat it, but WTAF Beamish?'

---

[5] Size XXXL.

28

'Official business, sir. We've come into some intelligence that can only be shared at the highest level.'

'I'm awfully busy. Couldn't you have passed a note to Lady Hortense, Cummings, or someone?'

'Neither the good lady nor your chief senior special adviser has the necessary security clearance.'

'Won't it wait? We're off on an enormously well-earned five-week holibob. That will take me up to Brexit day.'

'Whatever it is, I'm not cancelling,' said Young Symonds indignantly. 'It could be nuclear Armageddon or Lizziekins falling tits first off the Windsor battlements for all I care, but we're jolly well not stopping our holibob. Boris and I are fully committed to our holiday entitlements.'

'Speaking of Dommers, where the bloody hell is he?' asked Boris.

'He's tied up in waiting room number three, sir.'

'Tied up? Good lord, Beamish, what have you done with him? That Latvian cultural attaché is the most appalling bore.'

'Mr Palchuk is still cooling his heels in waiting room number four, sir,' Lady Hortense reminded him.

'Ah...excellent. Would you kindly advise staff that we'll be taking brekkies in waiting room number one?'

'As you wish, Young Master Boris.'

'Mr Cummings insisted on inspecting my service issue watch,' said Beamish.

Boris changed into his work clothes. Lady Hortense straightened his tie and combed his hair into a rough approximation of 'domesticated'. She tied his shoelaces strictly in accordance with the instructions in the appendix of Debretts. Suitably attired, Boris marched towards the door.

'Bumble, haven't we forgotten something?' said Young Symonds.

Boris jammed on the brakes.

'Ye Gods.' He checked himself in a mirror, studiously ruffled his hair, loosened his overlong Trump-inspired tie and hoisted his shirt out of his trousers.

'That's better, darling. I do so love the rumpled look with added crumbs,' said Young Symonds.

'Onwards and upwards, to the breakfast tables of England,' roared Boris and charged through the twin doors.

Downing Street Waiting Room #3

Boris, Young Symonds, and Beamish were served breakfast by the ministerial waste of space, and resident scouser, Downing Street sous-chef Esther McVey. Cummings rotated slowly from the ceiling fan.

'Are you alright up there, Dommers?' asked Boris.

'This is brilliant, Chief. I can see the entire room and visually plan the layout for the new feng shui furniture data metrics. I've spent too long thinking on my feet,' said Cummings enthusiastically.

Mrs McVey popped a prosecco cork and poured out a ration of grog.

'Thank you, Esther,' said Boris. 'What do you have for high table this morning?'

'It's the Downing Street classic breakfast, sir.'

'Pray remind me, dear girl.'

'Hard-boiled duck, hen, and quail eggs as you like them, sir.'

'Stonkingly superb stuff. With soldiers?'

'A full regiment, sir. Then we have honey roast ham, black pudding, oak smoked salmon, grilled fillet of sole, and Périgord truffle.'

'It sounds perfectly spiffy Mrs McVey. My compliments to the kitchen.'

'Thank you, sir. Will there be anything else, sir?'

'No, that will be all.'

'As you wish.'

She curtseyed and departed. Young Symonds watched her disappear.

'How I loathe that ghastly high-pitched accent,' she rasped venomously. Boris patted her hand.

'We must do our bit for diversity, Young Symonds,' he replied. 'It's all about levelling up, Northern powerhouse and ebahgum whatnot. People are always moaning that we are too London-centric. A temporary inclusion of all things Northern is a simple expedient for the times.'

'I know, darling, but Northern accents are beyond the pale. That screechy lower deck scouse accent is too much.'

Beamish took a sip of Prossey.

'One cannot argue with the woman's corkage. This is excellent.'

'Northerners do have their uses, Beamy,' said Young Symonds, amused.

'Now, what's all these jolly hush-hush shenanigans you want to tell us?' said Boris, getting to the point. He noticed Beamish's raised eyebrow quiver in the direction of his girlfriend.

'Never fear, Beamish, I've given Young Symonds full security clearance, and besides, she's better at concentrating on all this high-brow stuff than me.'

'Very well, sir. We've intercepted coded messages from the Chinese. It appears they have invented a brand-new virus in a place called Wuhan, injected it into some bats and now they're flying around infecting meat in a wet market.'

Boris shovelled a mash-up of black pudding and Périgord truffle into his mouth.

'Dear God, is there anything those dreadful people won't eat?' he said, spilling some revolting collateral damage down his third favourite tie. 'What's this got to do with anything? It can't possibly be more important than getting Brexit done, can it?' he asked.

'They're covering it up, sir.'

'Of course, they are. This is what those far-east Johnnies do best. Create an almighty SNAFU then spend all their time pulling the wool over people's eyes. Nothing new there.'

'They're worried about it, sir. Whistle-blowers have been arrested and threatened.'

'Quite right, too. Those types are always a frightful annoyance. No functioning democracy can afford to tolerate entitled nimbies. So, what do we know about this Chinese virus bat invention thingy?'

'We gather that it's an unusual type of pneumonia.'

'Is that it, Beamy?' yawned Young Symonds, finding it something of an anti-climax.

'This is highly disappointing, Beamish,' whined Boris. 'All this cloak and dagger stuff for a Chinese Sniffle. I thought it would be far more exciting.'

'I was thoroughly expecting to be on the edge of my seat,' agreed Young Symonds. She looked downcast. 'I was hoping you'd be telling us about bodies riddled with bullets, fake passports, and advanced combat skills.'

'Not forgetting lone wolf assassins,' put in Boris.

'Edge of the seat, whisked down to the bunker stuff, is what we're looking for, Beamy.'

'If you think for one nano-second that a Chinese Sniffle will in any way stop Young Symonds and me from frolicking in an idyllic, all-expenses-paid, tropical paradise for five weeks, you can think again.'

'Darling Bumble is right. Not letting us go on our holibobs would be absolutely beastly.'

'We're not stopping you going on holiday,' Beamish assured them. 'We think this potentially could be very bad news. The Chinese haven't breathed a word to the WHO, and our senior boffins suspect it could be transmitted from human to human.'

'What makes them think that?' asked Young Symonds.

'Because the Chinese say it's not transmitted from human to human.'

'So, what does this have to do with me?' demanded Boris.

'We need you to repair the special relationship before you jet off, sir.'

This startled Boris. He immediately disintegrated into a state of shocked disbelief.

'Heavens above, no. I can't do that. We've both moved on, and Young Symonds would take great umbrage at the very idea. Anything else I beseech you Beamy. This is all jolly underhand.'

'Not *that* special relationship, sir. We need a quick chat with Chinese President Xi. If we can repair the special relationship with our American cousins, then there's every chance Trump will make a call. It's the only way.'

'I'm sure the prime minister of Great Britain is eminently capable of calling the evil emperor himself,' said Young Symonds.

'You'd think, ma'am, but the Chinese president refuses to speak to him after they found an old clip of the chief saying that China was the cultural equivalent of a portable pop festival toilet.'

Beamish's tone was firm. He had his orders, and they were clear and unequivocal.

'We need you to make a phone call, prime minister, in the interests of national security.'

The blood drained from Boris's face.

'This is outrageous, Beamy. I think you should leave,' Young Symonds said. 'Don't do it, Bumble.'

Beamish coughed gently. 'Unfortunately, I must inform you that if you don't cooperate, then our beloved tabloid press might find out about about your holibob plans and who exactly is paying for your luxury villa.'

Young Symonds was appalled. 'This is nothing short of blackmail. It's utterly vile tosh, Beamish.'

'I'm sorry, ma'am, but my orders are to use every threat at my disposal to get the special relationship back on track,' said Beamish, with an air of non-negotiable finality. 'You'll need to call him directly. After lunch, sir.'

Minutes Later
Outside Number Ten

Beamish approached his bicycle, munching on a mouthful of Périgord truffle. Mrs McVey, bless her cottons, had thoughtfully spread it on a slice of sourdough toast. He rifled through his pockets and pulled out a set of padlock keys and Larry's folded map. He unravelled the paper and scanned the page. A secret beach? For five weeks? Out of reach of Her Majesty's security services? *Hmmm…curious and curiouser.*

The Next Day
Downing Street

A herd of Downing Street staffers scattered as Boris, clad in his trademark garish cycling gear,[6] ploughed through them on his trusty bicycle. Papers flew through the air; a laptop smashed on the floor.

'Charge for the guns,' yelled the prime minister as he shot out the front door at top speed. His legs pumped away like the pistons on Mr Rees-Moggs' steam-powered horseless carriage. Boris

---

[6] A threadbare TFL woolly hat, a helmet balanced precariously on top of the woolly hat, and red, blue, and white fish-patterned shorts.

always made important phone calls while riding his bicycle, despite the dire warnings from his personal secretary, Martin Reynolds. Marty was always anxiously bleating on about the risks from terrorism or, even worse, herds of mentally defective London motorists.

In return for restoring the special relationship, Trump demanded that Boris settle his bill for squeezing the thigh of the First Pay-As-You-Go Lady during a state banquet. Boris did his utmost to explain it was a traditional British greeting, but the Almighty didn't want to listen. It was seventy-five thousand big ones, or all bets were off, and not only that, but he demanded that Boris deal with the Scots.

Minutes later, the Big White Chief rocketed back through the door of number ten. Once again, several staffers, their peripheral technology, a group of bearded people carrying a petition, and a representative from the Latvian embassy enquiring as to the likely whereabouts of Mr Palchuck, were scattered to the four winds.

Boris skidded into the waiting room to find his chief senior special adviser lying on the breakfast table, surrounded by his junior flunkeys. They were engaged in an attempt to extricate him from Beamish's fiendish harpoon wire using bolt croppers and oxy-acetylene torches. Young Symonds was up a ladder, hammering in a nail for a new Banksy.

'So, all is well spiffingly spiffing in the wild west saloon, chief?' asked Cummings.

'Spiffingly spiffy,' replied Boris. 'I need to get Marty to put Trumpy's bill on expenses and the special relationship is back on track. He's agreed to email the Evil Emperor, and all we must do in return is bail him out from the clutches of Sturgeon's kilt munchers.'

'He's agreed to talk to Xi?' asked Cummings suspiciously.

''Fraid not, Dom. The great orange one only communicados with world leaders through Twitter or email. Helping him out with the rebellious clans will be a doddle.'

Cummings squirmed uneasily as a flunkey cut the harpoon wire from his ankles.

'What do you have in mind, Chief?'

'I haven't thought about it yet, but he was complaining about Sturgeon and the clans blocking the presidential hole.'

Cummings wasn't quite sure precisely what the chief was alluding to.

'The presidential hole?'

'On his golf course. They want to build a haggis breeding facility which would block the view.'

'The utter fucking planks. Don't they think of the thousands of jobs he'll create?'

Boris watched dispassionately as his chief senior special adviser climbed to his feet and allowed an underling to adjust the angle of his beanie hat to 'jaunty'.

Cummings rubbed his chin. 'This could be tricky, Chief. I can't see how you can get out of this one, even with an intensive, immersive course of blue-sky, feng shui, watsu massage thinking.'

'You should make them Lord and Lady Trump of Irn-Bru,' said Young Symonds brightly. She descended from the ladder. 'Give him one of those dodgy ancestry certificates, a coat of arms, and a personal fiefdom with the freedom to shoot sporran-crazed nationalists.'

'Whizzy idea, Young Symonds. What sayeth thou, Dommers?'

'Excellent as always,' said Cummings, putting on a brave face. He hated it when other people outflanked him with an idea he hadn't thought of. What did bloody Symonds know about the ancient art of blue-sky, feng shui, watsu massage thinking? Still, he had to show willing. He forced a smile and said, 'Don't you think the Molester-in-Chief will rumble our little Lord and Lady ploy, chief?'

'Trump? Not a chance. He's dumber than a doughnut hole.'

'It needs to look jolly antiquated and jolly professional,' chimed Young Symonds.

'I'm sure this wouldn't pose a problem for Beamish and our first-rate intelligence chappies. I'd go so far as saying that I've not been so sure of something since I upbraided the EU for banning prawn cocktail flavoured crisps,' snorted Boris, his snort mode now having engaged turbo snort mode. It was a well-known fact that the posher one is, the more robust and cacophonous the snort.[7]

Boris turned to Cummings. 'So that's it, Dommers, the special relationship is back on track. We have a Lord and Lady Irn-Bru, and we'll soon find out what's making these Chinese johnnies run around the place dressed like bats.'

---

[7] Rumour has it that Ancestry.com discovered that Jacob Rees-Mogg was 79% snort, 13% double-breasted suit and 8% umbrella.

'A great day, Chief. No one else could have accomplished so much.'

'Righto, so let's get lunch done.'

'We're off to Mamma Mia, darling Bumble.'

'What a stonkingly superb idea.'

'It's lunchies and a teensy bit of a meeting.'

Boris's inbuilt buoyancy sprang a leak. He felt instantly deflated.

'I'm not much of a one for meetings. They're a macabre pantomime where everyone looks at me as though they're fully expecting a decision or two.'

'We've no choice, I'm afraid, Chief,' said Cummings.

'Can't someone go in my place? I need a stunt double to perform these kinds of dreary chores. Matty has a Hancockgasm every time he hears the word meeting.'

Cummings tried to maintain an air of professional calm and patience. Dealing with the chief was far from easy at the best of times, never mind when this was a prime minister who wasn't massively interested in being a prime minister.

'I know, sir, but items one and two on the agenda require your most urgent attention.'

'What on earth is it? Surely the country isn't flooded again. If they're going to try to get me to declare a national emergency because some pea-brained, clog-wearing Northerners left their bath taps on overnight, they are sadly mistaken.'

'No, we've not been flooded.'

'Another outbreak of swine flu?

'No, it's not that either.'

'Don't tell me it's those annoying Neanderthal miner chappies again?'

'Indeed not, sir. There haven't been any miners since Mrs Thatcher had them all shot in the 1970s.'

'Well, that's one bit of good news. So, what prithee is it?'

'The Downing Street refurbishment and your holiday entitlement.'

'Christ in a tank top reading Thucydides on a bloody pogo stick.'

'Some interfering busybody has decided they are national security matters,' said Young Symonds.

'Quite,' put in Cummings. 'You'll need your important-looking briefcase number four, Chief. It's in stateroom three, behind Mr Churchill's old Chesterfield. The car arrives in five minutes.'

Downing Street State Room #3

After retrieving important looking briefcase #4, Boris felt somewhat aggrieved. There were times when he felt that Dommers was conspiring against him with his constant drip of bad news and inexhaustive lists of grisly prime ministerial tasks. His chief senior special adviser seemed to have forgotten their agreement that he'd only agreed to be PM until Brexit Day.

He gazed at a portrait of Churchill chewing a cigar, one of the few paintings that had escaped the attention of Young Symonds' ruthless art purge. What would the great man have done when he had to attend pointless meetings with mostly pointless people? He considered various options and concluded that strafing them from the cockpit of a Spitfire was not massively practical. Instead, his beady eyes fell on the cigar box that Churchill had captured from the Boers. It had remained there, untouched since the great man's death. It held pride of place on the table beneath the painting, beside the copy of the Magna Carta that Marty had used to confirm Larry's constitutional status. Perhaps a quick puff or two might help with the old decision-making process. He opened the box, selected a cigar, and lit up with Churchill's lighter. He took a lengthy drag and checked his reflection in the mirror. It certainly gave a gentleman a certain degree of gravitas. His reflective Churchill moment was rudely interrupted when Dom stuck his head around the door.

'Car's here, Chief.'

'Muchas Gracias, Dom. So, there's no way out of this meeting malarkey?'

'No way at all. Meetings are called in times of need, and Young Symonds saw the need to call this one.'

'Young Symonds?' spluttered Boris. He dropped his cigar on the fragile, tinder-dry pages of the Magna Carta, scooped up important-looking briefcase #4, and hurried after Cummings.

Sometime Later
Mamma Mia – Italian Restaurant

Boris, Cummings, and Young Symonds sat at a long table alongside various cabinet members. Beamish and Sir Simon Gass, the Chair of the Joint Intelligence Committee, joined them. Cummings casually flicked through the agenda while Boris wolfed down an enticing bowl of Kalamata olives in preparation for his linguine alle vongole. As a result, he was oblivious to just about everything. Only Sir Simon tapping the side of a dish of penne all'amatriciana with a large silver ladle snapped him out of his culinary reverie.

Young Symonds had called the meeting to discuss their choice of holibob destinations and the budget for refurbishing the Downing Street flat.

Young Symonds was *giving it some* within minutes of the meeting starting, as they say in modern urban parlance. She bristled with indignant rage, scoring at least a nine on the Princess Nut Nut chart.

'Fucking off Abroad is the divine right of a prime minister.'

'Agreed,' said Boris, pleased that his girlfriend had started on the front foot. 'If a prime minister can't fuck off abroad at every available opportunity, then what was the point?'

Beamish quietly polished off a gamberi arrabiata before pitching in with his considered thoughts.

'The problem, as the security services see it, is that every time the PM fucks off abroad, he refuses to answer his emails, do any work whatsoever and is invariably late back to the office on the Monday following his return.'

Boris wasn't having any of this. 'Utter tosh and fiddle-faddle,' he exclaimed, uncomfortably aware he was fighting a rear-guard action against the massed forces of holiday humbug.

'Certain intelligence has also come into our hands,' said Beamish.

Young Symonds was on her feet. 'What *certain intelligence* would that be then, Beamy?'

There was a noticeable tremor in the wing tips of Sir Simon's waxed moustache. A sure sign that something was afoot. In reply, and to Young Symonds' horror, Beamish brandished the top-secret Mustique beach map and flattened it out on the tabletop. Everyone left their chairs to crowd around and gawp while he pointed out various highlights with a silver fork:

- Main resort.
- Pool.
- Restaurant.
- Top secret escape route highlighted in red.
- Top secret quad bikes.
- Top secret beach – 1.5miles due east and out of reach of all electronic communication signals.

Boris's spidery hieroglyphics were instantly recognisable and irrefutable. He and Young Symonds had been caught bang to rights. Faced with such damning evidence, Boris pressed the bluster button.

'Oh, come on. It's only some joshing about. I had no intention of neglecting the responsibilities of high office,' said Boris.

He looked around the table. The expression on people's faces indicated otherwise.

'I do solemnly promise to do tons of filing in the mornings, answer the occasional email, and work on developing ladders and springboards to boost the UK economy.'

He mopped his plate with the remains of a bread roll and asked a passing waiter for an espresso.

Beamish leant forward. 'Based on our intelligence, we recommend restricting the PM and the First Bit on the Side to the UK borders, specifically a holiday bed & breakfast establishment conveniently located on Margate high street.

'WTAF, Beamy? Marbloodygate is not abroad. This is an absolute outrage.' Young Symonds raised her voice to wine glass shattering levels. She had the bit and a bit of langoustine firmly between her teeth.

'The brochure suggests that it's an idyllic rural retreat,' said Beamish, trying to sound reasonable and conciliatory.

'There's nothing quaint or idyllic about bloody Margate,' raged Young Symonds, sounding slightly less than reasonable and considerably less than conciliatory. 'Unless you happen to be a recalcitrant bin man who refuses to recycle dead rats.'

Sir Simon made a fist and rubbed it into his left eye. For some reason, whenever he came across Boris, he thought of Mrs May in a Spice Girls wig. It was time to weigh up the conflicting points of view. After debating whether to pour oil on his ciabatta or dip it in a small bowl of oil, he allowed the PM and the First Bit on the Side to go to Mustique for a maximum of two weeks.

Boris and Young Symonds were crestfallen, but it was better than nothing given the incriminating evidence. To placate the seething duo Sir Simon suggested that subject to a show of hands the Downing Street flat refurb budget could be increased to £200,000. After a lengthy, awkward silence with zero show of said hands, Boris shrugged his shoulders.

'Two hundred thousand pounds for a flat refurby these days is absolute chickenfeed. Hopefully, it won't affect anyone's budgets, moving forward,' he said with a well-practised air of degree of prime ministerial insouciance.

That did the trick. The slumbering cabinet ministers were galvanised into action. Hands shot up and Boris looked immeasurably pleased with the outcome.

'Motion carried, Mr Chairman. Time for dessert I believe.'

'Indeed. That concludes this meeting. Thanks everyone for coming in.'

Having moved on from the holibob, Beamish did have something else on his mind. 'This is all terribly fascinating, but I understood this meeting was also going to look at the new intelligence reports and the potential risks posed by this new virus from China.'

Sir Simon raised his head from his in-depth study of the Mamma Mia menu. 'I apologise if you were given that impression, but that wasn't the express purpose of this meeting. Domestic issues always take precedence over matters of national importance.'

'Dearest Beamy, don't be silly. I didn't call the meeting over some pathetic Sniffle,' said Young Symonds.

'Well, really, Beamish. This is bad form. It's hardly the time or place for a chat about this sort of thing. Can I tempt you with a panettone cheesecake?' asked Boris.

'It's absolutely sublime, old chap,' said Cummings, patting Beamish on the back. 'Now, who's up for a spot of entertainment?

I did ask the official Keeper of the Karaoke Machine to put in an appearance.'

An Hour or so Later
Downing Street

Young Symonds exited the Jag with regal grace and decorum. Boris staggered out behind her, a little wobbly on his feet. He'd spent most of the journey trying to work out why she had given him the silent treatment. He rightly assumed that words would soon be heated to 5000 degrees and freely exchanged.

He headed through the main door, singing 'Mamma Mia'. He stopped when Lady Hortense gave him her customary grade-three look of death, something she generally reserved for minor officialdom. Undaunted, he bellowed a hale and hearty 'Buornjorno' in her direction. Boris hastily patted down his hair, semi-tightened the knot in his club tie and made his way unsteadily towards stateroom #3 for some unfinished business with that Churchill cigar.

A thick pall of smoke and a shrieking fire alarm greeted him, along with a frantic personal, private secretary. Dear Marty appeared to be carrying the smouldering remains of a self-immolated chicken.

'Cripes on a fudge stick, Marty. I've told you a hundred times not to use Deliveroo.'

Marty dutifully came to a standstill. 'It's not a takeaway, sir. Some hideous oik set fire to the Magna Carta.'

'The nation's history up in smoke. What's to be done?'

'It's burnt to a cinder. The damage is irreparable.'

'Cheer up, dear boy. If those *Repair Shop* chappies can mend an entire shop, surely a few mouldy sheets of old parchment and a beeswax seal can be fixed up in a whiff of the old jiff.'

Marty visibly brightened.

'I have a Kindle communication device, sir.'

'That's the spirit, dear boy. Download a new Magna Carta, print it out, and nobody will notice the difference.'

'Mum's the word, sir.'

'Mum is the very essence of the word.'

With that, Marty sprinted off in the direction of the front door.

Christmas Day, 11.35 p.m.
Downing Street Bedroom

Young Symonds paced the room, fists clenched. Her eyes blazed in anticipation of an outbreak of upper crust violence. Boris stood at the window, dripping in sweat. The atmosphere could best be described as tense. Sex, as so often happened in their turbulent relationship, had failed to grope its way onto the day's agenda. Young Symonds' pregnancy and an inexplicable (to his mind) surge in anti-Boris hormones had put paid to that. For Boris, this was familiar territory: finding himself with an irate, temperamental, preggo female on his hands and dropped slap bang in the epicentre of an ongoing sexual imbroglio. The old man had counselled him on the estimable virtues of keeping it in his trousers, and the wisdom of that was now painfully loud and clear. Hypothetically speaking, he knew Young Symonds was on the verge of detonating her limited-edition Harvey Nicholls eco-explosive vest.

One of the great unanswered questions of his life was: how do women become instantaneously preggers whenever he happened to drop anchor in their home port? How did he freefall into their siren clutches? It was a recurring theme, guaranteed to disrupt the serenity of high office at a moment's notice. Once Young Symonds announced it was preggo o'clock, he suffered premonitions of impending doom. Nothing was more pending on the doom front than the realisation that from now on, his life would be like navigating the local high street, knowing the council had installed random trap doors every few yards. He couldn't afford to get thrown out again, especially now if it meant that Young Symonds left him high and dry, there was every chance she could become PM. Things were a taddly bit complicated as he was still married to that Wheeler woman, or the Wheeler-Dealer as he dubbed her. That would need sorting out at some indeterminate point in the future. For now, it could be safely kicked into the long grass to fester on the trusty old back burner.

Young Symonds cut through the fog of tension with a voice like the jagged edge of a smashed Wetherspoons beer bottle on a Friday night.

'How did Beamy get hold of the map?'

Boris quailed, stammered, and ruffled his hair in the face of her barely controlled wrath.

'I agree it's all a bit fishy,' said Boris, trying his best to avoid her thermonuclear stare. Quailing was never a solid defence against wrath, barely contained or otherwise.

'I'm reliably informed that you suggested my moniker, "First Bit on the Side," was your idea, darling Bumble.'

'Jolly early on, Sweetpea. I believe we were only seven shags into our relationship when they ambushed me for a code name.'

'Is that the best you could come up with?'

'I thought Top Totty was a little demeaning.'

In one lightning-fast move, Young Symonds grabbed a Denby stoneware coffee mug and hurled it in his direction. It missed his head by a fraction of an inch and smashed against the wall.

'That puts paid to the imperial blue set,' observed Boris.

'FFS, Boris. This was our chance. To fuck off abroad, away from this poorly furnished rat trap for five weeks and sit out the month until Brexit day. I dreamt of us hanging out with our toes in the sand whenever we felt like it. You being prime minister is bad for our health. I don't want to bring up a child in a world contaminated by weirdo special advisers in woollen beanie hats. Do you want to be stuck in this depressing hellhole for the rest of your life?'

'Hardly, dear girl, I wanted to be world king. Becoming prime minister was only the first step.'

'The first step to what? Penury? You said so yourself – the money is rubbish. Chickenfeed, you called it.'

'How did I know I'd have to give up a glittering journalistic career and stop writing my books?' He was uncomfortably aware that his infinitely better half had edged closer to him.

'Oh yes, the bloody writing. Your book on Shakespeare. What is it called? *Ye Merry Wyfes of Bloody Boris*. Well, that will fly off the shelves about as fast as *Harry Potter and the Bucket of Used Condoms*. I'm sure the Nobel prize committee will be devastated.'

'Mrs May earns half a million pounds from her speeches alone, never mind the royalties for her Kenyan dance CD.'

This stopped Young Symonds in her tracks. 'People pay good money to listen to the world's most boring crone?'

'She's the Glastonbury of losers. Some people like that sort of thing, like old school friends and the criminally insane. Fear not, Young Symonds, when I stop being prime minister, we'll be rolling in it.'

He kept a wary eye on Young Symonds and side-stepped around the marble-topped coffee table.

'This is your fault, and now we have Beamy skulking around the place, peeking and aiming his CCTV cameras into the most intimate crevices of our lives.'

'The intelligence services have been enormously diligent in impressing on me the utmost importance of security.'

'Well, they would, wouldn't they? They've nothing to do all day apart from spy and pry.'

'What are you talking about?'

Young Symonds held up a small wire contraption.

'A listening bug, Boris. I found it inside one of my thongs. The devious dirtbags have been sniffing around my knicker drawer. That must be how they knew about the map.'

She was close enough now to reach out and deftly flick him hard on the nose.

'Not the nose, you know I hate that.'

Despite the pregnancy, Young Symonds was surprisingly fast and somewhat furious.

'I'm sure we'll find a way through this. Let's examine the balance sheet. They've agreed on the budget for the refurby, so whatever we buy, we can take with us,' he said.

WHOOSH. He narrowly managed to dodge a lethal uppercut. He ran past her. Sadly, he'd mistimed his run. Young Symonds stuck out a strategic foot. His vast bulk took him steaming into one of her reviled ex-Mrs May, John Lewis sofas. It immediately collapsed in protest. He howled in ego-damaged indignation.

'I promise we will get through this,' he said cheerily. This was classic Boris. He'd mentally brushed aside all objections, practicalities, and shortcomings. Now he had to focus on the familiar outline of Young Symonds heading straight towards him at a substantial rate of knots. The last thing he remembered was a fleeting glimpse of a fist-shaped fist flying in the imminent direction of his left eye.

26 December
Downing Street

The most optimistic, feelgood Prime Minister of Great Britain, the colonies, and an industrial estate slightly to the left of Luton, Boris Johnson, emerged from the Downing Street lift, nursing a black eye. He was also stonkingly resplendent in an ill-fitting powder blue safari suit and an ill-matching, ill-fitting, and generally ill Hawaiian shirt. Jacob Rees-Mogg followed, attempting to carry two cabin cases and a suitcase the size of HMS *Ark Royal*.

Rees-Mogg sweated profusely and removed one of his top hats. He manoeuvred the case into position a few feet away from the Downing Street front door. He'd drawn the short straw earlier on, after hoping that some grubby little sycophant like Hancock would get it, and now had the unenviable task of breaking bad news to Boris.

'I'm awfully sorry, sir, but one is led to believe that the prime minister's aircraft, Hairfarce One, has been blagged by her Royal eminence.'

'Her Madge? This is an outrage, Moggy.'

'Indeed, Sire. Ms Patel has all the details.'

The lift bell rang, and Home Secretary Priti Patel came out pushing an ornate hotel-style luggage rack, weighed down with all manner of shlocky designer suitcases – Versace, Gucci, Burberry, Hilfiger, Lidl, etc. Young Symonds sat cross-legged on a mountain of zebra-print luggage with her eyes glued to her phone and a huge pair of Boris-cancelling headphones clamped to her head.

'Patel, what's going on with Hairfarce One?' demanded Boris. Patel saluted and stood rigidly to attention. She'd do anything for her hero, but pushing his entitled little minx around seemed strangely undignified.

'Begging your pardon, Chiefy, but sadly, the Defender of the Faith has had to take an emergency flight to Balmoral.'

'Of all the nerve.'

'She left handbag number 397 in the ensuite of bedroom 109. Her Royal Madgeness can't live without it.'

'Very well, and how do you propose we flee this festering junk heap of a country, Priti?'

'I've sequestered a Ryanair Flight.'

'Ryan…bloody…'

Boris was appalled. Ryanair was the epitome of 'no-frills, keep taking the pills' transportation. Only the steadfast shoulders of Mr Rees-Mogg stopped him from face-planting the Downing Street pavement.

Villa Whiff-Whaff, Musty

Boris cut a solitary figure as he swept up half a ton of broken glass and smashed plates from around the pool area of his luxury villa. Whiff-Whaff contained the five essential e's of a corkingly superb holibob:

- Exclusive
- Executive
- Extremely expensive
- Eminently luxurious.
- Eejit free zone – no journos, paps, or bloody red boxes.

His great friend David Ross, the founder of Carphone Warehouse, had laid on the whole thing. All rip-roaringly, stonkingly marvellous, but his head was still packed with murderous thoughts about Mr O'Leary, the frightful boss of the peerless money-grubbing airline Ryantightarseair.

The flight to Musty was utterly horrendous. Young Symonds went totally psycho nut-nut over Priti Patel's dubious choice. She'd been traumatised as a child when Mummy and Daddy forced her to fly somewhere foreign on the beastly airline. They'd ended up in the wrong airport, miles from their destination and had to travel via a disgusting mode of public transport popularly known as 'a bus'. What made it worse was the mind-crushing re-alisation that there was no first class. Even after all these years, the thought of sitting near ordinary people, going about their ordinary business and who were quite incapable of telling one end of a pony from another, filled her with extraordinary dread. The humiliation had been too much to endure. Imagine recounting the unimaginable horror fest to her posho friends, Athena, Cortina, and Thomasina Smythe-Smith-Smythe? She had no intention of revisiting that sordid avenue of shame.

'Ryan-fucking-air. Are you shitting me, Boris?'

'No dearest, Lizziekins commandeered Hairfarce One, and well, here we are.'

'No inflight entertainment, the girl at check-in looked me up and down as if I'd absconded from a Turkish drug prison, and they charged me for their so-called food.'

'We can claim it all back.'

'A Ryan-bloody-air burger and chips. It's not exactly the tasting menu at Le Gavroche. What a bloody mess, and all after letting our secret map fall into enemy hands.'

'I agree, the paltry fayre on board was as insubstantial as it was distasteful. Seriously below par.'

'They ran out of crisps and coke. How can you run out of crisps and coke? As if that weren't enough the cabin crew were utterly vile. Did you hear that dreadful man tell me there was no first class when I insisted on being upgraded to first class? The impudent little shit. It's barbaric and he didn't even know who I was. You're the prime minister, for pity's sake. Do something.'

The unpalatable truth was that Boris wasn't sure what to do. He'd made the mistake of packing his executive Churchill decision-maker in the hold luggage, and now he was flying by wire. Young Symonds was scorn personified, and he had no rational answer.

'Since when is Lizziebloodykins more important than me? In case you didn't notice Boris, I have more power than her. Even Larry the Cat has more power than her.'

Under the terms of the English constitution, Young Symonds was perfectly correct on this front. The English constitution is not written down because no one could write in the olden days, and access to word processors was tricky at best. The result was that people tended to make things up as they went along. As for the cat business, since the English Civil War, a cat has been permitted to override the will of the monarch at all times, although due to a bureaucratic error made by George III back in 1765, it does have to put this in writing.

'Leave it to me, Sweetpea. I'll soon have this little misunderstanding under control.'

'Little misunderstanding!'

KA-BOOM. That was the big bang moment. Young Symonds went ballistic and attacked the glassware and crockery.

Boris gazed at the collateral damage he'd swept into a corner. He remembered her words about taking responsibility, and it was time to put his plan to placate the poor girl into place.

His chance came at breakfast, a sumptuous multi-course spread laid on by Louis Philippe, a top Michelin chef, who Marty had cunningly smuggled onboard. There were even drinks with umbrellas sticking out of them. Such extravagancies, Boris knew, were the internationally recognised standard for high-quality haute cuisine.

Young Symonds was lounging in her sarong. She idly flicked through the pages of one of her many designer tattoo magazines while contemplating talking her infinitely worse half (IWH) into having the Joker one from *Batman*. He certainly had the necessary acreage for a large tattoo. That would be dead sexy, she thought, suddenly aware of a small velvet-covered box being prodded across the table.

'Qu'est-ce que c'est ca, darling Bumble?'

'Seek and ye shall find.'

Young Symonds opened the box. Her eyes twinkled in delight.

'An engagement ring, my angel. It's divine.'

'Having you referred to as the First Bit on the Side is getting seriously on my low-hanging undercarriage, darling. I thought it was time we had a stab at the betrothing business, and I can officially appoint you as the First Fiancée. I take it you'll be happy marrying me despite the temporary difficulties with Mr O'Leary's wretched travel service.

'The BBC announced his execution this morning.'

'Quite right, too. Head on a spike outside the Lidl in Streatham. Let that be a lesson to all those who think they can inflict poor service on their superiors. That will teach the uncouth layabout not to lay on vodkas, first-class seating arrangements, or televisual entertainment on an aircraft. It beggars' belief.'

'Oh darling, this is wonderful news; of course, I'll marry you. I'm sorry about my fit of pique and all that broken glass and crockery. Just think, Bumble, I was sorely tempted to give you the old heave-ho. So, what will you do about the Wheeler Dealer?'

'We'll need to keep it all jolly hush-hush until she signs the bloody divorce papers. I don't see her problem. I mean, how hard can it be? All she has do is sign her name. Job done.'

'Let's celebrate with a game of beach volleyball.'

'We'll get Cummings and Brutus Govicus involved.'

'Did you have to bring them out here? Govicus the traitor is about as coordinated as a rabid badger, and Cummings smells like rat stew.'

'No choice, I'm afraid. Someone must attend to the affairs of state while I have officially fucked off abroad. No need to worry. I'm not getting a briefing until the third of Janners. Besides, I can't play solo in a safari suit. They're well known for cramping one's style.'

'How brief is the briefing?'

'It will be a brief mini-briefing followed by a full de-briefing with the emphasis fully on the 'brief.' I've warned Dom against mountains of emails and anything longer than one hundred and forty characters.'

'A la Trumpy?'

'Indeed. I have a lot to thank the cunning old fox for.'

January 2020

Villa Whiff-Whaff, Musty

January began for Boris with another sunny day in the tropical paradise of Mustique. Mid-morning, and he was already up and about. He surveyed the wreckage of a small Spanish fleet of model sailing galleons lying at the bottom of the wine glass shaped pool. Sir Francis Drake had triumphed again. Huzzah!

Young Symonds was on full alert, listening to Mumford and Sons belting out something folksy and awful down her outsized headphones. She preferred to keep her eyes firmly shut to reduce her exposure to the sight of Bumble wandering about the place with his shirt tucked into his shorts. She took a sip of Lustau Pedro Ximénez San Emilio Sherry and lowered her outsized sunglasses, the better to avoid the sight of Cummings heading towards them in his government issued Speedos and correctly angled woollen beanie.

'What ho, Chief. It's already been a good morning judging by the shipwrecks at the bottom of the pool.'

'Top of the morning, Dom. That's the armada put to flight. This is how we dealt with Europe in the old days. A curse on their EU directives. So, tell me, do we have any schemes or devious machinations afoot?

'At all times. I had an excellent blue-sky, reiki, chakra, watsu massage sesh with the new team over breakfast on the beach, during which we fully optimised the wide learning structures and analysed the empiric data flow.'

Boris nodded sagely, as he always did when Dommers veered into nerdish crackpot territory.

'The new team?'

'The old one failed our diversity benchmarking test, I'm afraid.'

'You couldn't ask for a better place for a fist-pumping meeting with the troops. It's absolutely superb. I feel, Dom, like I get so much more done here. I don't have to read anything, sign anything, or do very much at all. When I'm in Downing Street I'm constantly forging iron for Hephaestus and he's put me on minimum wage.'

Young Symonds opened her eyes and spotted Cummings.

'Morning Dom.'

'Morning First Bit on the Side.'

'Not anymore.'

Cummings took a seat next to Boris. He hunched forward and reached for a glass of Sherry.

'I'm all ears.'

'First fiancée now, Dom.'

Young Symonds showed off her engagement ring.

'Congratulations. We must keep it jolly hush-hush, what with the Chief still being married to the Wheeler Dealer and all that.'

'Correctamondo Dom.'

'I've also taken the liberty of catching up with a couple of international incidents that have raised their heads while we've been away, Chief.'

'Incidents? I expressly refused to allow any "incidents" to interfere with my holibob.'

'Holibobs take precedence over "incidents", every time,' said Young Symonds.

'The First Fiancée is spot on. Nothing must jeopardise the holibob, Dom. I'm in a deep state of zen wellness relaxation here. Psychologists have known for many years that a prime minister of the realm needs his hols. I can't carry on head down, reading all sorts of reports and briefings forever. It takes its toll. I'm sure you can appreciate that,' said Boris.

'Apologies, chief and ma'am chief. There's nothing to worry us whatsoever. This is more of a touch base, organic, artisanal, micro-briefing. I don't want to keep you away from the beach.'

'OK, just tell me the worst.'

'That Chinese Sniffle our friend Beamish was wittering on about has turned out to be a thing.'

'Cripes. Do we need to do anything?' said Boris. 'I'm ready to be bloody, bold, and resolute as my friend Macbeth would say.'

'No need for that, Chief. The merest hint of doing anything implies doing something. We certainly don't want to give that impression and I would strongly advise being on the same hymn sheet as other world leaders. Evil Emperor Xi, for example, doesn't seem to give the proverbial monkeys about it, and apparently, his spokesman instructed Trump to do something unspeakable via email. He finally informed the World Health Organisation that some unidentified bat pneumonia thingy was on the loose but it wasn't spread through human transmission. That was on New Year's Eve.'

'He had time to do that on New Year's Eve? What were we doing on New Year's Eve, Young Symonds?'

'Far too busy to be doing paperwork, that's for sure. We watched *Elf*, had a conga around the pool, quaffed champers by the gallon, and started a knees-up with Athena and Cortina.'

'I can't imagine sunny boy Xi having a knees-up or watching *Elf*,' said Boris.

'What a saddo. Firing off missives to the WHO is like total party-pooper land. All this not spreading through human transmission sounds like Chinese waffle bollocks to me, darling,' said Young Symonds.

'This is all jolly hush-hush, Sweetpea, and we're supposed to be projecting the image that we are keenest of Sinophiles.'

'It doesn't make sense, is all I'm saying. I don't know much, but I do know that pneumonia is spread through germs. So, it must have come from someone.'

Boris looked impressed. 'Sometimes, Young Symonds, you come across as a genius.'

'The other incident, Chief, is that the Americans have blown up an Iranian general.'

'Typical. If they're not shooting each other, they're blowing up someone else. Is it a jolly serious blowing up? One presumes they have more than enough generals to go around. Again, do we need to do anything?'

'Absolutely nothing, Chief. Shadow Home Idiot Thornberry is ranting to the press that you're sunning yourself on a beach, drinking pomegranate martinis, and not paying attention.

'Typical demented jibber jabber. That woman couldn't cobble together the ingredients of a cheese sandwich."

'Who in their right minds would cut a God-given holibob short with two days to go?' Young Symonds interjected.

'Exactly, Young Symonds, exactly. That woman is a third-rate also-ran in the wits department.'

5 January
Return to Downing Street

A cavalcade of fifteen black Range Rovers (fourteen of them groaning under the weight of Young Symonds' monogrammed designer luggage) threaded its way through the streets of London. Young Symonds and Boris stared morosely through the windows.

'This is terminally depressing,' observed Boris. 'Small wonder the Luftwaffe gave it up as a bad job.'

'It's awful.'

'Thank your lucky stars First Bit on the Side. I'm sorry – First Fiancée. We'll be cracking off to sunnier climes as soon as it's politically expedient,' said Boris with one of his customary optimism bombs.

'How can you be so relentlessly upbeat and plucky, darling? If you'd been a bit more careful with that bloody map, we could have fucked off for five weeks instead of a measly two-week drudge fest with a group of escaped convicts. Now, they'll always find you wherever you are. You'll be camping on the far side of the moon, and a bunch of brain-dead paparazzi on a moon buggy will hove into view above a crater. It's all rather like that *Taken* film. Someone like Leslie Neilson or Beamish on his bicycle will always hunt you down and find you, using their unique set of horribly irritating skills.'

'I think you mean Liam Neeson, darling, and it's only until the end of January. After that, freedom and the amply rewarded lecture circuit shall be upon us,' Boris replied gently as the car nosed into Downing Street. 'Ah, the slave labour camp doth beckon.'

They stepped out, and Boris instantly came under fire from a salvo of impertinent questions yelled out by the herd of ill-educated reporters:

Is it true you were sunning yourself and shotting martinis while the entire Middle East exploded, Mr Johnson? (*Guardian*)

Did you read any emails while playing beach volleyball, Mr Johnson? (*Times*)

Do you realise you are the actual prime minister of the UK? (*Telegraph*)

Is it true you can't be bothered that there's a brand-new disease infecting China? (*Independent*)

Oi, First bit on the Side, did you get your first bits out? (*Sun*)

A Piffling Trifle of English Minutes Later
Downing Street

Once safely inside, Mr Rees-Mogg and Priti Patel fussed over the happy couple.

'A most hale and hearty welcome back, sire. One must apologise for the appearance of these uncouth vagabonds. Shall I prepare the boiling oil?' said Rees-Mogg. His eyes kindled like a swarm of fireflies.

Boris felt that any conversation with the Moggster was like a Delorean time jump back into the early nineteenth-century. Still, he did his best to keep up.

'I feel that would be most agreeable, Moggy. If any of the bounders overstep the mark, you know what to do.'

'Very good, sir. In the meantime, I'll instruct the constables to give them a light beating with their trusty bamboo sticks.'

'Most convivial, I must say. Pray instruct them to wade in at will.'

'Can I help?' enquired Young Symonds.

'That's an exceedingly generous offer, Young Symonds. However, it may tarnish your reputation as a lady of good standing if you're seen in Her Majesty's media meting out a jolly good thrashing to the lower orders, no matter how well deserved,' replied Rees-Mogg.

'Sound advice, thank you, Jacob.'

'My pleasure, ma'am. Will you be promenading this evening, my leige?'

'I fear not. We are somewhat fatigued by our travels.'

'Of course, sire,' said Rees-Mogg, with a gentle inclination of his head.

A faithful retainer escorted Young Symonds up the stairs to the flat while Boris headed for his study. An aide held out a silver tray full of printed emails. Boris walked straight past him. He continued his march through Downing Street, ignoring another aide holding a silver tray full of non-urgent junk mail. Then there were various aides proffering more silver trays of pizza delivery mailshots, leaflets from the local North Korean fast-food takeaway, flyers from estate agents, and a handwritten note from Terry Bennett & Sons. Judging by his leaflet, Mr Bennett was the semi-literate, local guttering and drainage entrepreneur. He went to some lengths to inform his readership that he was currently working in the area and was happy to give the householder a quote free of charge.

In his study, Boris looked aghast at the sheer weight of paperwork on his desk. Cummings slid in behind him, followed by Marty, who had a pair of trademark files tucked neatly under his arm.

'That's going to keep you busy, sir,' said Marty.

'You told me you'd delegated low-grade piffle to the underlings, Dommers,' Boris cried in alarm.

'Well, there's been a blizzard of highly purposive, data-driven, strategic developments,' said Cummings, carefully adjusting his expression into a rough approximation of empathy. 'Marty, if you'd care to step into the breach.'

Marty knew his way around the Whitehall menagerie blindfold and had considerable expertise in diffusing Downing Street contretemps. Boris's private secretary loathed special advisers with a passion and reserved an exceptional level of suspicion for jumped-up oddities like Cummings, whose raison d'etre was sniffing around the corridors of power to see what they could scavenge. Still, he had a job to do.

'Sadly, the chancellor, Spreadsheet Saj, reduced our underling quota by thirteen point five per cent,' he explained, 'and the underlings' primary task was to sift through the junk mail. In the absence of said underlings, due to austerity measures, the prime minister is expected to open all his Downing Street correspondence, including all digital whatnots, sent on electronic contrivances.'

'Why is everything always thirteen point five per bloody cent?' demanded Boris.

'That's Spreadsheet Saj for you,' put in Cummings. 'I warned you, he's trouble that one.'

'He also does all the sums,' said Marty.

Boris grabbed a bundle of papers at random.

'So, what's all this? Trade deals that will transform us into Global Britain?'

'Sadly not, Prime Minister. This is all Brexit-related red tape, although most of it is generated here in the UK.'

'But I was always told that it's the EU that churns out all the red tape.'

Marty and Cummings shook their heads.

'That's not the case. We generate it by the proverbial ton. Remember all the health and safety stuff and nonsense?"

'Brussels, clearly.'

'Whitehall, Sir,' said Marty.

Boris sank uneasily into his wooden captain's chair, the one with an inbuilt swivel mechanism. Marty had told him it helped with acute depression. Looking at all that paperwork, he wasn't sure how effective it was.

'My God, Dom, I need a bloody holibob!' exclaimed Boris.

'You've only been back five minutes,' said Cummings.

Marty attempted to alleviate the situation and opted for a more diplomatic route. 'I can see it's daunting, but we can't put it off for more than a couple of days. The country grinding to a halt for the sake of some pizza leaflets and a guttering flyer is not a good look.'

Boris grunted. A Boris grunt was well known to kick start his mental spinning bingo cage and scatter any pertinent facts and figures to the periphery of his brain.

'I'll jump into the paperwork trenches on Wednesday.'

'I'd highly recommend looking busy in the meantime, sir,' replied Marty, trying not to sound over-critical. 'Particularly when entering and exiting Downing Street.'

'How on earth do I do that?'

'It's quite simple, sir.'

Marty took the files from under his arm and handed them to Boris.

'Two files under the arm in public places, at all times. It will give the impression that you mean business. One red and one black.'

Cummings observed Marty in full flow. It took Boris several attempts to configure the mechanics of retaining the files under his arm for more than thirty seconds, but he triumphed in the end. There was no doubt about it. Despite being a Whitehall mandarin and therefore fully worthy of a chief senior special adviser's disdain and contempt, Marty knew what he was talking about.

7 January
Downing Street

Boris brooded at the small table in the Downing Street study. Part of him was still back in Mustique, rewinding to that fateful last throw on the beach quoits game. He kept running it over and over in his mind even as he stared at Matt Hancock's gormless mouth flopping up and down. It was as if the mouth operated entirely independently of the face. He scrambled furiously for a suitable comparison. A boiled halibut sprang effortlessly to mind. Still, Matty was relentlessly enthusiastic. Here was a man who'd been known to interrupt himself by involuntarily raising his own hand during a meeting. This was someone who couldn't believe his luck, a perpetual head boy who had somehow landed on his feet. Now, he had an important cabinet post as health secretary. His dream had come true, and by some inexplicable sorcery, he was briefing the PM about a brand spanking new Chinese virus.

Boris took a stab at sounding as if he were vaguely interested. As always, his razor-sharp intellect quickly marshalled all the salient facts. 'So, our Chinese friends have brewed up some bat bug in a fish market and are hell-bent on blasting it into outer space?'

'Not quite, Chiefy. What's happened is that the Chinese invented a new virus in some godforsaken dump called WooHoo, and now it's escaped and is on the warpath.'

'Righto. Should we be worried about a Chinese Sniffle?' Do we need to start digging trenches?'

'Officially, the worry level is at a record low. The Chinese aren't worried about it; our European neighbours are only officially slightly worried about it because President Xi says it's nothing to worry about, and the WHO isn't particularly worried because the Chinese have told them the Europeans aren't worried about it. We find ourselves occupying the mid-worry ground, as it were. I had a brief chat with the Mad House staffers. President Trump is so worried about it that he's gone to his Mar-a-Lardo resort to play golf, and Mr Putin is indulging in bare-chested outdoor pursuits this weekend.'

'Beamish mumbled something about intelligence reports suggesting it could be part of his Melania botox avoidance strategy.'

'Yes, Chiefy. Anyway, I've taken the liberty of arranging a cabinet meeting to discuss our Brexit strategy and upcoming trade deals.'

'Ah yes, some proper business to occupy the keen political mind. I hope it's not going to be too early, Matty.'

'Half past eleven. There's plenty of time for you to have a vital nutrition break, Chiefy and make sure you bring your Oyster card.'

'Whatever for?'

'As part of levelling up, the cabinet meeting will be held outside Downing Street. We're travelling on an underground train and a London bus for the return journey.'

'Whose bright idea was that?'

'Your chief senior special adviser, Mr Cummings.'

'Dear God, I take it we still have Mrs Krysinski's magnificent tea trolley to look forward to on the return leg?'

'Indeed, Chiefy.'

7 January, 11.30 a.m.
Tube Train, Westminster Station

The train was crowded. The cabinet team were all present and dangerous. Armed with her size six hockey stick, Priti Patel went through her wellness relaxation regime by barking orders at a ragtag group of asylum seekers. They wore silver thermal blankets and sat cross-legged on the floor. Boris jumped on board, wolfing down a croissant he'd grabbed from Pret. He took his seat in the middle of the carriage.

'Morning troops,' he tootled. 'Any ideas why the train seems to be grounded?'

Sgt. Major Patel was on it without blinking an eye. 'Severe delays,' she barked, then saluted Boris and clicked her highly polished heels. 'Bloody rain, sir.'

'Rain?

'Entirely the wrong type. Bloody useless country, sir. No bloody backbone. Deport them all, I say. Like I did with my parents last Christmas. That will teach them to moan about our

British weather. I made the hopeless duffers take the citizenship test. Neither of them could name a battle won by Henry the Fifth, or knew that "Swindon" was a sexually transmitted disease.'

Boris's eye caught sight of the shivering migrants.

'Who exactly are these people you've brought along today, Priti?'

'Immigrants, sir. I nabbed them personally at zero-five thirty hours while out on patrol with my gunboat.'

Boris pumped his fists, and as if through divine intervention, the train moved off. 'That is stonkingly awesome dedication, Priti. I hope everyone is taking notes.'

The rest of the cabinet joined in with a chorus of 'for she's a jolly good fellow.'

Boris stuck up his thumbs and bulldozed straight into the day's agenda.

'So, everyone, the order of the day is Brexit, which, as we all know, is building to an intoxicating climax. Let's have some zoinking killer updates on all these stonkingly stupendous trade deals we've got simmering on the front burner. Liz?'

'It's The Truss if that's ok with you. Chiefy?'

'Absolutely, The Truss. My bad.'

'I started it all off with The Saj, Chiefy,' whined Spreadsheet Saj, who was feeling left out.

'I love The Saj, but my expert advisers tell me Spreadsheet Saj is far more professional.'

Spreadsheet Saj briefly met the smug, unwavering eyes of Cummings. He had his suspicions about which particular expert adviser had swayed Boris, but this was a battle he could fight another day.

Hancock fidgeted. He had to get ahead of the pack somehow. 'If Liz is The Truss, then from now on, I want to be known as The Cock.'

'No need to worry, Matty, we're all ahead of you there,' agreed Boris.

The Truss scrunched her face up in that disconcerting way politicians have when they unexpectedly find themselves in the spotlight.

'With Brexit, we need to cut, burn, slash, and deregulate, then cut, burn, slash, deregulate again, scupper the EU, chuck human rights in the bin, and get the country back to where it belongs.'

The Truss's words electrified the cabinet. This was what they wanted to hear. Libertarian drivel ripped from the pages of the Tory bible.[8] Cut, slash, burn, and deregulate were their commandments. The ministers rose as one from their seats and erupted in a round of applause. The side effect of this was a certain amount of wobbling and grab rail grabbing owing to the train's velocity.

Boris beamed with delight.

'Bang on the nail, The Truss.' He patted her on the back. There was something reassuringly dull about dear old Liz. Listening to her had the same soporific effect as one of Young Symonds' Yoga Flute relaxation CDs. He admired her dogged loyalty

---

[8] *Brittania Unchained* - just after the chapter about Thatcher being omnipotent.

despite the Almighty's curious decision not to install any discernible traces of personality during his groundbreaking creation process.

'I can reveal that we now have the following deal in the bag, and it's an absolute spiffer. With the Republic of Moldova, I've agreed on a no-tariff agreement on fridge magnets, Cornish pasties, Wedgewood pottery and potted plants, worth over ten thousand pounds.'

'Ten thousand pounds? That doesn't sound much in the way of fridge magnets, pasties, espresso mugs, and spider plants,' Raab pointed out. 'Anything with the USA, China, or India so far?'

Boris groaned inwardly as an outward groan didn't feel right. Trust Raaby to futz Liz's circuits and leave her in a state of partial paralysis just as things were going so splendidly. For some reason, he had a fleeting image of the First Secretary of State with demonic horns protruding from his temples. He blinked and settled back into listening mode. Fortunately, Matty was on hand to deflect attention away from Liz's catatonic eyes rolling back in their sockets.

'Eminently splendid work, The Truss. How are they for fridges, by the way?' asked The Cock.

Slowly, almost imperceptibly, The Truss's neurons rose from the dead and she spluttered back into life. 'Mrs Thatcher, the great restorer of inequalities, quite rightly stopped this great country of ours us making useless things like fridges. Fridge magnets are, I'm afraid, the absolute nearest thing. We have crack teams of artisanal organic free-range fridge magnet makers, and their skills are recognised the world over.'

The Cock rose to his feet as the train lurched into a station. 'Three cheers for all our British free-range artisan organic fridge magnet craftsmen and women, of course.'

The cabinet joined in with a raucous 'Hip Hip Hooray'.

'While we're at it, let's have a round of cheers for Mrs Thatcher,' suggested Priti Patel, brandishing her hockey stick. She jumped to her feet, threw off her hi-vis vest, pulled her shirt over her head, and ran around the carriage like a footballer celebrating a hat trick. To a crescendo of cheers, she took a last lap and slid across the filthy floor on her knees.

Boris wiped the sweat from his brow. 'Superb and awesome stuff there from The Truss and Priti, I think we'd all agree,' said Boris. 'We can now enjoy a leisurely jaunt back to Downing Street, courtesy of one of my specially hired Routemaster buses, accompanied by Mrs Krysinki's renowned tea trolley. Now, is there any other business?'

It was tradition for a PM to ask for 'any other business' when, in fact, 'any other business' was the last thing on said PM's mind and was code for 'no other business'. Most cabinet ministers couldn't be less interested in 'any other business' if they tried. With no 'any other business' on the horizon, it was incumbent on the PM to dismiss the team to go about their business. The Cock however, was not a man to stand by tradition. The mornings 'no business' was interrupted by a light cough. Steely cold eyes slowly manoeuvred towards The Cock. If he was to break with tradition and raise an 'any other business' hand, they'd be doomed to a journey back to Westminster listening to the most boring man in Christendom. He raised his hand, opened his briefcase, and removed a wad of papers.

'The Chinese Sniffle, Chiefy. They do seem to have brewed it up out of nothing, and we need to review the national risk level.'

Raab glared at The Cock. Given half the chance he'd happily stop the train and lash the demented lunatic to the tracks.

'Where is it now, Matty?' asked Boris.

'It's low, but it should be slightly higher.'

'Slightly higher than low?' rasped Cummings.

'Yes, I'd suggest the next thing up from low. To show we have it fully under control. We've not heard much from the Chinese.'

'I'm seeing the Chinese ambassador in a couple of weeks for the Downing Street traditional lion dance. I'll butter him up and see if he's heard anything. For now, we'll say the risk level is unknown as it stands?'

Cummings shook his head.

'I'm afraid that won't wash, Chief. Unknown makes it sound like we don't know what we're doing.'

The Cock stuck up his hand for the twenty-seventh time.

'Mr Cummings is right, Chiefy. We've assessed the risk of unknown things, and from our extensive records and data, the threat level posed by the unknown remains unknown. As it is unknown, we can safely assume that the risk level should rise slightly from low to moderately low and the unknown will therefore become known.'

Boris and the rest of the cabinet looked baffled. Still, when bafflement was on the menu, the only thing to do was go along with it.

'Thanks for clearing that one up, Matty. So, let me get this straight – the threat level of unknown things is moderately low.'

Cummings was taken aback. The Chief was on the cusp of grasping something, and he wasn't talking about various parts of a lady's anatomy. That's the thing with The Cock. When he went full-on *Rain Man*, he could come out with remarkable flashes of insight. It made a refreshing change from wanting to punch him in the face.

The train stopped, and Boris climbed to his feet. 'All change, folks. We're sallying forth back to Westminster on one of my stonkingly superb routemasters.'

'Everyone on the buses lower deck, please. The Chief and I have an urgent matter of national security to discuss on the upper deck,' said Cummings.

'National security?' hissed Boris as he and Cummings left the train.

'Trust me, Chief.'

Boris dutifully followed his chief senior special adviser. Trust? Well, there was a first time for everything.

Ten Minutes Later
Open-Topped Tourist Bus

Having a national security meeting on the top deck of a London tourist bus, slap bang in the middle of winter, was a wheeze straight out the Cummings Nobel-prize winning book *Blue-Sky Thinking for the Feng Shui, Watsu Massage Thinker.*

'What happened to the Boris Bus, Dommers?' asked Boris.

'Mix-up in the reservations department. Sorry about that, Chief.'

'There's no LED lighting and the climate-controlled ventilation system is somewhat rustic.'

'It's all we could get at short notice.'

'I feel like I'm being dragged off to the local dump in a builders skip.'

Boris eyed Dom. This whole 'get everyone out of Downing Street' business was deeply suspect.

'Let's change the political landscape, Chief,' the balding Svengali had said when he first mooted meetings out of Downing Street. 'I need to get you away from the Downing Street noise and unnecessary Groupthink.'

Boris wasn't entirely sure what he meant by 'noise' or 'Groupthink', but, whatever, it sounded like a jolly good idea to get away from it. However, if changing the political landscape for the poor man's version of *Snowpiercer* was what Dommers was aiming for he was quite happy moving meetings back to their more traditional non-levelling locations. Thanks to Dom, he found himself on top of a rickety, freezing cold tourist bus, surrounded by a gaggle of Japanese tourists heavily armed with 36-megapixel cameras and state-of-the-art 48-megapixel anoraks.

Cummings squeezed up beside him. The bus braked as it lurched around a corner and propelled a portly man from Okinawa onto Boris's lap. The Gods were looking kindly on him, thought Cummings. If that wasn't authentic feng shui, chakra, watsu, karma, then God knows what is.

'So, what's up, Chief?'

'What's up? I thought this was a matter of national security.'

'It was one of my masterful ruses. I needed to get you away from the cabinet. My razor-sharp feng shui senses told me that the PM mindset was in a state of fundamental distraction and needed a holistic reset with yours truly.'

'Okay, level with me, Dom. My popularity has never been higher, and Brexit is bang on track. I want to make sure my exit strategy is likewise oven-ready, as it were.'

'Everything is in hand, Chief. The party grandees have an alternative lined up. Apparently he's something of a reluctant volunteer, and needs to attend an intensive training course, but they assure me it's all systems go.'

'This is the right decision I'm making, isn't it? Quit while I'm ahead, then rake in the doubloons on the speech circuit, or write a stonkingly whizzy column in *The Mail*.

'Absolutely. I'd also be looking for an exit strategy if I was PM. It isn't the best of hands to be dealt. It's like buying a house without bothering to complete a survey. You start with a dream and end up with unwanted subsidence and neighbours in hoodies who drive white vans, and call everyone 'mate'.

They shuddered at the thought and stared at the leaden sky, contemplating these words of wisdom. The Japanese tourists were busily engaged in taking photographs of The Shard, a hideous mile-high slab of glass and concrete, surgically removed from that paragon of classic architecture, Dubai, and shat out on the wrong side of the bloody river. Boris hated it. A giant cock and balls would have been more appropriate.

'Time to rejoin the troops, Chief,' said Cummings, breaking the moment.

Boris stomped down the stairs to the lower deck, leaving the Japanese to feast on the London Skyline horror show, and sat opposite The Cock and Raab.

The Cock stuck up his hand.

'Was that a pre-meeting meeting with Mr Cummings, Chiefy?'

This was prime The Cock and an outbreak of The Cock, even at this time of the day, was not for the faint-hearted. It was like being in the same room as a constipated baboon.

'No, Matty, we were discussing pressing affairs of state.'

'May I briefly establish the rules? I take it we are moving from the pre-meeting meeting into resuming the initial meeting itself. It's just that I'm taking the minutes, and it's important to get these things tickety-boo.'

'Indeed, we are. Is everyone ready?'

There were nods of agreement around the bus and before discussing the Sniffle, a point of order was raised vis à vis the disappointing lack of an onboard tea trolley service.

'I regret that I've had to deport Mrs Krysinski, the chief, senior, special tea lady,' admitted Priti Patel. 'It was due to an unforgiveable Oxford comma violation on her right to stay application.' Patel loathed Oxford commas even more than immigrants. Not only that, but the tourist bus organised by transport wallah, Mr Schnipps, wasn't equipped with a retractable ramp for wheelchair/official tea trolley users. Priti was pleased to announce that she'd outsourced the bus catering service to Deliveroo, thus protecting British jobs and adding value for the taxpayer.

'Appalling. I never suspected anything,' said a deeply chagrined Boris. 'Mrs Krysinski's morning egg and bacon sandwiches were the finest things in breakfast history.'

'Bona fide objets d'art,' agreed Spreadsheet Saj.

'No more homemade marmalade?' groaned Raab. 'Or damson jam on Tuesdays. That just about made being a politician worthwhile,' he said, dabbing his eyes with a tissue.

The Cock was a bag of nerves and tongue-tied.

'It's just well…you know, with the Sniffle business.'

'We know what, Matty? Come on, man, spit it out,' demanded Boris.

'I think we might have to do something.'

The cabinet briefly coalesced into a state of traumatic shock. Raab, Patel, and Spreadsheet Saj sat there with their tongues lolling out while two thousand gigawatts of pure, unadulterated, apoplectic panic ripped through their nervous systems. It was like some horrendous homage to *The Green Mile*. When they recovered, and the wisps of smoke curling out of their ears wafted away, the tension was palpable, as tension invariably is.

'Do something?' hissed Boris angrily. 'You told me there was nothing to worry about. I'm meeting the Chinese ambassador for Chinese New Year, so we can't do anything that the Chinese could in any way interpret as offensive.'

'What are other far inferior countries doing?' asked Raab.

'Italy is considering banning flights from China, as are the Americans, and there are rumours about temperature testing for airport arrivals,' replied The Cock.

'Banning flights? Cripes, that would be a classic bad look. It sounds like they are surrendering to the Sniffle. No mettle, no spunk. Dommers, a penny for your thoughts?' asked Boris.

Cummings thoughtfully stroked his chin with his thumb and forefinger. The cabinet hunched forward in their seats. Agog.

'Only one thing for it, Chief. We dust down a traditional internal UK government strategy for the next week or two.'

'Deploy the time-honoured Do Fuck All policy,' said Raab, nodding his head in admiration.

'Bang on, Raaby. That could buy us some quality strategic thinking time while I work out some flow charts and pick up new whiteboards,' said Cummings.

Spreadsheet Saj harrumphed and tapped away on his laptop. He highlighted something in red and sat back, sucking the air through his teeth.

'Unfortunately, we have exceeded the Downing Street whiteboard budget.'

'Surely not!' exclaimed Boris.

'Whiteboards are mission critical,' Cummings bristled indignantly; hackles raised to at least a level eleven, quite possibly a twelve. 'The government cannot function without them. You should not have this item on the austerity spreadsheets.' He gave Spreadsheet Saj a withering look and folded his arms.

'Yes, I'd whip those off if I were you,' agreed Boris. 'Juggle some figures and take a few quid from somewhere else.'

Spreadsheet Saj looked from one to the other. A look of dismay swept across his face. Everyone seemed to be against him, and this lot could turn against him faster than a ship full of outsourced Somalian pirates. At some point, he would need to think before he spoke. Tread carefully, very carefully indeed, thought Spreadsheet Saj to himself. He tapped his keys. A spreadsheet with the heading WELFARE appeared. He adjusted some figures and hit SAVE with a flourish of his arm.

'The Treasury is happy to announce that an inflation-busting thirteen point five per cent has increased the Whitehall whiteboard and stationery budget. This will, of course, protect British jobs for hardworking British people.'

Boris clapped his hands.

'Excellent work, Spreadsheet Saj.'

Like all cabinet ministers, Spreadsheet Saj was bereft of humour. Still, he thought, this might be an opportune moment to sally forth with a faint trace of a smile.

Cummings looked pleased. He'd never been too keen on Spreadsheet Saj. Far too too clever, far too oily, and far too bald for his own good. Some of these cabinet ministers needed reminding who was boss from time to time. His attention turned to The Cock. The custodian of the nation's health clearly had something on his mind.

'The Do Fuck All policy, Dom?'

'Yes, Matty. We need to bring it out of hibernation,' said Cummings, who sat back and folded his arms behind his head.

'Which is what, exactly?'

'It's quite straightforward, old chap. We buy a large pile of sand and bury our hands in it for a week or two.'

'But the Chinese…the virus…flights from China?' gabbled a dumbfounded The Cock. He was in many respects like a puppy, including the compulsory electronic collar the security services made him wear when he was away from parliament. Cummings waved his hands dismissively.

'We need to show we are taking decisive action by not taking any action. The classic double bluff.' Boris grinned appreciatively.

'Wouldn't the Do Fuck All policy be more effective if we buried our heads in the sand rather than our hands?' said The Cock.

The table glared at him as if he'd released the most prodigious cloud of noxious personal gas emissions since an entire Alaskan Walrus colony consumed the contents of a washed-up shipping container full of chickpeas.

'Leaflets,' he blurted, more as a random pressure release than anything else.

'Are you alright, Matty?' asked Boris, taken aback at the blurt that had distracted him from Priti Patel's freshly manicured union jack nails.

'Yes, leaflets. For my money, I'm not sure if putting our hands in the sand fully covers us for doing fuck all. I recommend that we go full-on head-in-the-sand.'

This surprised Cummings. Maybe there was something about The Cock that he'd missed. He sat bolt upright.

'Go on, Matty, I'm intrigued.'

'By definition, if we bury our heads in the sand, that alone could be construed as showing that we are doing something. The act of head burial would, therefore, be seen as taking a kind of action in itself. Thus, the passive act of handing out leaflets would counteract the previous action, and thus, we successfully take an action without actually taking an action.'

'I'm beginning to like this, Matty. What exactly do you have in mind?'

Cummings wanted to see where The Cock was going with this. He was nothing if not hyper-enthusiastic and had certainly grabbed the attention of the finest chief senior special adviser in all the land. That, for no other reason, had to make it all worthwhile.

'We print out leaflets with NHS on them. We station teams of workshy, good-for-nothing, lackadaisical NHS workers to dish them out to all arrivals at Heathrow. We could give them a phone number to ring if they feel a taddly bit woozy on their flight or have been exposed to a dreadful Baz Luhrmann musical on the inflight entertainment system.'

'No one would know that we have taken the action?' said Cummings.

The Cock nodded and smiled sheepishly.

Cummings was a step or two ahead of the cabinet and at least five steps ahead of Boris. Priti and Spreadsheet Saj couldn't believe their ears. They both made mental bets on how many years this had successfully wiped off The Cock's life expectancy. Cummings stood and pointed his index fingers at The Cock, making violent stabbing motions in his direction. The Truss's face had taken on the appearance of a three-week-old scrambled egg, and

The Cock looked as if he was about to spontaneously combust in a spectacular display of radioactive cinders.

'This is what I'm talking about. That is classic out-the-box, blue-sky, reiki crystal, watsu thinking. Sensei would say it's the very essence of doing fuck all.'

Taking his cue from Cummings, Boris climbed to his feet. 'We can kick all the Sniffle cans into the long grass. By the time we lift our heads out of the sand, this Sniffle business will have blown itself out. Stonkingly whizzo stuff, Matty.'

Cummings was also impressed.

'Thanks to you, Matty, we now have head-in-the-sand with added leaflets. I'd always pencilled in *limited* in my assessments of you. Still, now I know you have the capability to deliver the key deliverables to our key stakeholders and take them to the next key holder level.'

With this, Cummings rang the bell and marched off the bus, taking Boris with him. The cabinet was left utterly boggled. They gasped for air, trying desperately to understand what the great one had just said. The cogs in The Cock's brain clunked slowly into place.

'What just happened? Am I still alive?'

Raab put an arm around his shoulder. 'A great performance. It seems you're destined for higher things.'

'I think Mr Cummings and Chiefy really like me,' said The Cock, somewhat breathlessly.

'Don't push it, Matty. It's more than your life's worth. Better just order up the sand,' said Raab.

22 January
Downing Street – Rose Garden

Two weeks of radio silence later, the huge pile of sand in the centre of the garden shook. It rumbled and came alive with a series of minor tremors. Boris and a gaggle of cabinet ministers emerged shaking the sand out of their hair. Due to a natural process of complex sand molecule retention, Boris had more than most. The master of the rumpled, dragged through a hedgerow backwards, across the M25 motorway, then back through the hedgerow again look, was in an ebullient mood. He was pleased to finally breathe again after enduring a face full of sand for two weeks.

Cummings sat in the long grass, surrounded by numerous tin cans filled with orange blossom and lemongrass incense sticks. He had adopted a classic yoga pose, his head covered in correctly aligned feng shui, watsu acupuncture needles. To the casual observer, he bore a striking resemblance to the Pinhead character in *Hellraiser Eleven*. He muttered several metaphysical incantations for the benefit of the moving forward blue-sky-thinking Gods.

'What a top-hole policy that is Dom. We jolly well smashed it,' said Boris.

'It's the classic all-time politician's ruse, Chief. Guaranteed to throw people off the scent. I'm pleased we changed the hand-in-the-sand strategy back to the head-in-the-sand strategy. The Cock, for once, was right.'

'I think we've underestimated him. Anyway, we've successfully managed to do nothing for a couple of weeks and the Sniffle will now be in full retreat.'

Cummings ran a thumb along his second favourite cheekbone. 'Absolutely. We ran the country with zero government interference. This will go down brilliantly in all those annoying red sewage farm areas.'

For some reason, Boris felt more than a little uncomfortable with the great Svengali's liberal use of the word 'we'. Of course, he liked Dom and, indeed, was mightily dependent on him for a great many things, including the stupendous wheeze of camouflaging the contraceptive machine in the third-floor bathroom. However, and this was an epically large billboard-sized however, he did feel something of a gnawing sense of unease at the way Dommers seemed to think that he was equivalent in status to a democratically elected prime minister. Especially one as universally adored as he was. The 'we' word troubled him. It didn't feel right. At the very least, the 'we' issue was a level three botheration. He might need to discuss it with nanny over a late-night cup of hot chocolate. Fortunately, thoughts like this didn't float around too long in the boiling ether of Boris's brain. His synapses, as per normal, surrendered early doors before moving onto something far less demanding.

'Sometimes, Dom, I don't know what I'd do without you.'

'You'd have to go back to being Lord Mayor, Chief. You know, sort out electric penny farthing rental schemes with Moggy, zip wire in reverse across the Thames juggling flaming swords, enthusiastically rub yourself up and down against ladies' silver dancing poles, and all that sort of thing you have a natural flair for.'

Boris scowled as The Cock staggered out of the sand. An aide holding a Starbucks coffee cup handed him a bundle of papers. The Cock hastily flicked through them and hurried over to Boris and Cummings. He was enjoying himself.

'This is exciting. It's all rather like the Great Escape. There's been a jolly hush-hush meeting of SAGE in the Starbucks at Kings Cross station, Chiefy,' he said, shaking what appeared to be the contents of one of the great dunes of Erg Chebbi from out of his trouser legs. The Cock slobbered with all the enthusiasm of a Doberman Pinscher celebrating its first mouthful of an Amazon Prime delivery man's left buttock.

'I have the top-secret minutes of the jolly hush-hush SAGE meeting at the Kings Cross branch of Starbucks.'

'SAGE? Why are they having meetings? Hasn't the Sniffle been sent packing?' asked Boris.

'Apparently not, Chiefy. Some oiky professor type called Ferguson said he thinks there have been thousands of cases that the Chinese aren't telling us about and expressed a concern there are lots of flights coming into the UK from China. A couple from Dudley who were waiting for their crème brulée brown sugar frappuccinos wanted to know about the Sniffle. They also quizzed him about 'R' numbers,' said 'The Cock.'

Boris rocked uncomfortably on his feet. This had the unfortunate side effect of generating a mini sandstorm in the hair department, successfully half-blinding Dominic Raab who stood downwind.

'Where the hell did these people get this R number whiffle?' he demanded.

The Cock rifled through his notes.

'It was in the newspapers.'

'Are they officially part of SAGE?'

'The papers?'

'No, dammit, the coffee swilling inbreds from Dudley.'

'It doesn't look like it – they were waiting for a train, the three thirty five to Birmingham New Street. After some heckling, Professor Ferguson let it slip that *we'd* given the NHS the leaflets to hand out at airports.'

'Professor Bofferson? I thought SAGE was so secret that even those in it didn't know they were in it,' said Raab.

'So, not an innocent mistake by the sounds of it. I don't trust these bloody boffin wallahs, and these people waiting for a train sound suspicious,' said Cummings.

'If the meeting was jolly hush-hush, perhaps they were undercover,' said Boris.

'Good point, Chiefy,' said The Cock. 'We should get Beamish out to investigate.'

Cummings' expression darkened. The Cock had overstepped the mark again. His internal mechanism for ignoring protocol and ruffling the feathers of chief senior special advisers was exceedingly well developed. Cabinet ministers were under strict instructions to go through the chief senior special adviser's office rather than report directly to the PM.

'But it's true, Chief. It must be investigated. Here, read the reports for yourself.' He held the paperwork out to Boris. Apart from Churchill, *The Telegraph* and Shakespeare, Boris never read anything, especially when it was government related.

'Sorry, Matty, but as CEO, I delegate reading things to my crack team. Priti, if you would be so kind,' said Boris.

Priti Patel was busily engaged in dragging Spreadsheet Saj out of the sand mountain by his legs. Once she heard her name being called, she immediately let go and ran over to the prime minister. Left to his own devices, Spreadsheet Saj was powerless. He attempted to claw his way out with his clipboard, but the sand wasn't beaten. Keen to retain its shifting sands reputation, it rose menacingly behind the hapless Chancellor. He screamed. Priti turned her head and watched him being sucked back inside. She had bigger fish to fry, and impressing the chief was more important than providing emergency chancellor rescue services.

'Morning, Chiefy, what can I do for you?'

'Have a squizzer through Matty's papers, would you? I need a second opinion.'

'Rah-Rah!'

She snatched the papers out of The Cock's hands and flicked through them.

'They're genuine, Chief. The Cock is correct. There is a Sniffle outbreak in China, which we know about. Chinese people are coming here in their plane loads, which we knew about, these people from Dudley were in Kings Cross Starbucks waiting for their coffee, which we didn't know about, and Professor Ferguson is part of SAGE, which we also didn't know about.'

'Thank God we took an action by not taking an action.' Boris sounded relieved.

'Fortunately, because of our esteemed and valued Do Fuck All policy, we can all safely say that none of us have been officially briefed about all this. Well, we knew about it but didn't know about it, so we can officially deny everything,' said Cummings.

Pleased with his machinations, Cummings churned all this over, including the likely consequences and the consequences of the likely consequences. This is why he was enormously well paid. He was doing a job that no one else could possibly do, under any circumstances, without any consequences to himself.

'Look, Chief, whatever happens, all we have to say is that we are the best-prepared nation on the face of this earth for any kind of eventuality and, indeed, the best nation for anything whatsoever. Frankly, I don't see what else anyone could expect the government to do,' said Cummings.

The Cock bit his nails. 'I'm supposed to be saying something in the house tomorrow. We have developed a test for the Sniffle.'

'Do other far inferior nations also have a test?' asked Boris.

'We're one of the first, Chiefy.'

'There you go,' said Cummings, 'hit them with that. It's absolutely genius.'

The Cock puffed himself up. 'The UK has developed a test for the Sniffle. I have to say, that sounds totally spiffy.'

'The Sniffle won't know what's hit it,' said Boris. 'Our testing will be like a barrage of anti-aircaft guns. We'll blow it out the sky if it decides to rampage across the Channel.'

The Cock was still anxious. 'People are talking about "rapid case detection", whatever that means.'

Boris attempted to put him at ease and dropped a playful handful of sand in his breast pocket. 'You'll be fine. Like Dom said, tell everyone that we are the best-prepared nation on the planet and add this testing malarkey into the mix'

'Relax, Matty,' said Cummings, 'we'll have a brainstorming session and a pre-commons meeting, followed by a pre-commons blue-sky, feng shui, watsu massage briefing.'

Boris was bursting to say something. His face reddened as it always did at times of great excitement.

'If they're talking rapid case detection, Young Symonds was magnificent on the luggage carousel at Mustique International. I fully take on board that ninety-seven per cent of the luggage was hers, and admittedly, it was all monogrammed with C.S, but she directed operations and had people running all over the place. That included the entire Mustique police force.'[9]

'There you go, Matt,' beamed Cummings, 'we're already half-way there – nothing to worry about whatsoever.'

'Do you want me to rescue Spreadsheet Saj, Chiefy?' asked Priti, pointing to a pair of legs struggling for traction in the heap of sand.

'Something tells me you already know the answer to that one, dear girl,' he said helpfully.

Pie & Mash Shop, London's East End
Official Downing Street Levelling Up Work Meeting

The Cock loved meetings so much he'd decided to have a pre-work meeting, meeting with himself, in eager anticipation of the

---

[9] Officer Murray Wilmott and Buster the dog.

main meeting, organised by Mr Cummings. As this was a work meeting away from Downing Street, in the spirit of levelling up, he'd taken the opportunity to level up and dress like a local. Thus was he resplendent in full cockney pearly king regalia, including a pair of rather fetching Cor Blimey trousers. They smelt like a flea-ridden kebab house cat, but needs must.

Matty placed shiny brass nameplates on the opposite sides of a rickety vinyl-covered cockney table. They were emblazoned with the legend MATT 1 and MATT 2. Matt sat in the MATT 1 chair.

Transcript of unofficial solo The Cock pre-cabinet meeting, meeting:

MATT 1: Morning, everyone, thanks for your time to-day. We can safely assume that matters vis-à-vis the Chinese Sniffle are, as they say, gathering momentum.

Matt left the MATT 1 chair, ran around the table and sat at the MATT 2 chair. This continued each time he needed to alternate between them.

MATT 2: Morning, Prime Minister. I have a tricky question.

MATT 1: God, it feels bloody marvellous being called prime minister.

MATT 2: Indeed, Prime Minister, but you've not answered the question.

MATT 1: You've not asked me a question yet, Matt.

MATT 2: Ah…spot on, as always, Prime Minister.

MATT 1: As prime minister of this great nation of ours, I'm always open, in the name of democracy and transparency, to any questions, tricky or otherwise.

MATT 2: Thanks for being so jolly reasonable, Chiefy – sorry, I meant Prime Minister. I'd like to know who the 'they' you referred to in your opening statement are.

MATT 1: 'They?'

MATT 2: Yes, 'they.' As in 'as they say.'

MATT 1: Not sure I'm following you, Matt.

MATT 2: It's a simple question, Prime Minister.

Matt slumped back in the MATT 1 chair. MATT 2 was beginning to sound like Laura Kuenssberg.

MATT 1: Bollocks.

A Pre-meeting Meeting

As his pre-cabinet meeting hadn't gone well at all, it dawned on The Cock that he might not have what it takes to be PM. Maybe it was more than simply being in meetings, pre-meetings, strategically balancing files under his arms to look important, sporting a generally dishevelled look, and being massively overweight. Although he adored meetings, he might not be as terribly good at them as he thought. He remembered meetings with Daddy in the family firm. He once put his foot in it over one of Muriel's spreadsheets and had found himself busted down to photo-copier supply clerk (grade five) on the ground floor within a week. All this thinking on-your-feet shenanigans invariably caught him out. Not his sort of thing at all. There was lots of stuff to discuss in the cabinet meeting about the Chinese Sniffle, but he wasn't sure if he was ready.

'Morning Matty, nice and early, I see.'

Christ. Mr Cummings loved meetings even more than he did. A love that was, frankly, borderline sinister. An acknowledged spiritual master of the whiteboard, he couldn't imagine the Svengali of Spin being stumped by a question he asked himself. He thought about asking for a tip or two, but Cummings was a certifiable oddball. How would this be interpreted? Would he be calm and rational? Or was he more likely to go into one of his full-on Jack Nicholson-esque mood swings a la *The Shining*? Dom's temper was notoriously incendiary. No, he couldn't afford to take any kind of potential career-damaging risk. Play his cards right; there was no reason he couldn't be prime minister one day. That would put the HR losers in the family software business firmly in their place. The thought of it filled him with pride.

For now, he'd have to bite his lip, continue polishing his head boy badge, and keep his fingers crossed that the great one wouldn't notice or suspect anything. After all, he had no intention of returning to a career that revolved around ensuring Muriel's stationery cupboard had an adequate supply of cyan printer ink.

Cummings' caustic tone cut through his thoughts. 'Big meeting today, Matty. Give us a hand rearranging the chairs, would you?' He tapped the chairs with a chakra tuning fork. 'The feng shui winds have changed direction.'

The Cock looked around. The chairs appeared to be perfectly normal. They stood on the floor and were generally chair-shaped, which benefitted the humble surroundings of a traditional pie and mash emporium.

'They look perfectly fine and dandy to me.'

'Fine lines, Matty. It's all about the fine and lines. That's the difference between success and failure. They are dependent on vibrational frequencies which leaves them hanging precariously on a knife edge of perception.'

'Does it depend on how fine the fine lines are?'

Cummings somehow held his inner thoughts in. He felt like a sommelier, standing in front of some ill-educated, working-class bellend whose idea of fine wine was a glass of Lidl Chardonnay and had unfortunately survived to tell the tale.

'Not when Mercury is in Venus, and the chakra fault lines have shifted. I wouldn't expect a non-mystic to know that, but trust me, it has realigned, and the tolerances are minimal.'

'Don't we all just sit facing East with the windows open and blasts of icy cold air freezing our knacker regions?'

'No Matty. Until the fault lines realign, the room is out of balance. It must be restored so that we are in harmony with the natural order of things. Namaste.'

'Namaste, indeed. Do we care about the natural world? I mean, is it awfully important?'

'Everything is connected, Matty. If we can't move the furniture into its optimum position, we risk losing control of the energy force.'

He saw the blank look on The Cocks' face.

'More importantly, it means potentially jeopardising the deep connection between the cabinet and the Tao of Boris.'

'The Tao of Boris?' The Cock was drowning in a tsunami of Cummings-speak.

'Spiritually speaking, Boris is like a river. We are his tributaries and naturally gravitate towards the heroic new messiah. Our very being morphs into him. His way becomes our way. Whatever he thinks, our bodies and minds are one. This is the great confluence, the coming together of the five elements.'

'All this coming together sounds a bit off colour, old chap, even in this liberal, enlightened age we're living in.'

'Don't worry about that now, Matty. Let's get some of this furniture moved. They'll be here in a few minutes. Grab hold of the table.'

'It must weigh two tons.'

'Put your back into it. The damn thing needs to be angled.'

He produced his state-of-the-art laser protractor. After some considerable scraping on the spit and sawdust floorboards, the table was arranged at a Cummings-approved angle.

'Great work, Matty. Do you see how the leader will now have a clear line of sight to the door and the outside world?'

'Looks plain old wonky to me if I'm perfectly honest,' replied The Cock, eyeing the table dubiously.

'You need to get your head around out the box Blue-Sky thinking. We are talking critical level feng shui. Having the desk at this angle represents our leader's spiritual vision.'

Boris had a 'vision?' This was news to The Cock.

'You mean he can now see out the door, along the corridor to the cockney toilets?'

'It's not just to the toilets, Matty, but what the toilets represent.'

'Which is what, exactly?'

'The bottomless well of his all-seeing leadership.'

The Cock wasn't sure about this. Not sure at all. Power was rushing to Dom's head. He seemed to be turning Boris into a cult figure, and there was one thing he was sure of: Boris was not yet a complete cult. Still, he was just about savvy enough not to let his festering doubts surface.

'Absolutely splendid, Dom, splendid.'

He inadvertently patted Dom on his back. As soon as he committed this heinous act, he was instantly transported back to Daddy's software business for a split second. There he was, shivering in a pool of his own making, being ceremoniously busted down to photo-copier supply clerk (grade six) after patting Muriel on her back. Then, as now back patting was a massive tactical error. Dom was seconds away from erupting in a fit of splenetic fury. Only the arrival of Priti Patel with a freshly captured tribe of handcuffed cross-channel migrants in tow prevented The Cock from being reduced to a pile of ashes by an inter-continental ballistic laser protractor.

Post Pre-Meeting, Meeting
Also Known As The Actual Bloody Meeting

Due to the angle of the table, it made for a tight squeeze. Priti and her migrants had to clamber over it. She took her seat while a burly security guard made the migrants sit cross-legged against the wall. They wore hi-vis vests, monogrammed 'PP' name tags, and were all soaked to the skin.

'Looks like you've had a busy morning, Priti?' Dominic Raab sat opposite the Home Secretary. He ran an approving eye over her Primark jackboots and the gaggle of shivering migrants.

'Rather, Raaby. I was up at zero four hundred hours this morning. I had a quick polo chukka, then took the old gunboat out on patrol. We ran over a dinghy at zero six thirty and found this bunch of ungrateful scumbags doggy paddling in Her Madge's English Channel. Rah Rah!'

'Good for you. As always, I'm a ceaseless admirer of your self-less dedication to protecting our borders.'

'Thanks, it's never easy.'

'At this rate, you'll soon be turning Kent into a refugee caravan park.'

Priti's eyes flashed in anger.

'Refugees!' She spat it out. The R-word, not to be confused with the Sniffle R-word, inevitably triggered all manner of un-controllable psychotic reactions.

'They're not?

'"Refugees" means status. Status means benefits. Benefits means access to our world-leading NHS queues, and a two-for-one discount on tins of Beluga caviar at the nation's food banks.'

She regurgitated a mouthful of croissant at the very thought.

'You're right, dear girl. I'd quite forgotten the difference.'

'How the hell did you find out about Kent?'

'One of those nice people in the handcuffs and your splendid hi-vis vests told me.'

'Honestly, these people can't be trusted with anything.'

'He told me he was a doctor in his country.'

'They all say that. Find me an Uber driver who isn't a brain surgeon, theoretical physicist, or ex-president of Albania, and I'll make you an honorary member of my fox-hunting society.'

'Excellent point, PP. Ah, here's the chief, now.'

Boris made a regal entrance. Cummings had recharged the batteries in the PM's favourite bow tie to break the ice. It spun at high speed and emitted a mesmerising display of multi-coloured flashing lights. Cummings installed him in the feng shui, watsu, chakra chair. A bikini-clad Esther McVey, her mouth firmly sealed with anti-Scouse tape, whiff-whafted him gently with a large palm tree frond as if he were some important foreign pomegranate [checks notes] – potentate. This was the kingdom of King Boris, and all was well.

The Cock handed out cigarette packets. On the back were the notes from the SAGE meeting summarising everything they knew about the Chinese Sniffle. Boris waved his arms around, signalling that the work meeting was kicking off.

'Hail fellows and well met. I hope we're all spiffy and in the rudest of health.'

Despite the generous helpings of crispy cockney pie, peas, and liquor handed out by the pie and mash shop staff, no one seemed enthusiastic. Priti Patel attacked the mushy peas with gusto, resulting in a loud squelching sound. Boris looked around the tables. The energy levels had flatlined. Dom's genius plans for taking Downing Street into the big wide world was proving disastrous for morale. By jingo, he was going to have to rally the troops.

'Come on,' he exhorted. 'We've almost got Brexit done. It's the only policy we've been interested in since attempting to preserve the Ottoman Empire. Let's have a glorious show of fist-pumping to get this meeting off to a jolly positive start and show Johnny Foreigner that we plucky Brits mean business.'

This was enough to kick-start the troops. They stood at their tables and engaged in a burst of frenetic fist pumping. Boris was happy with all this. Positivity and optimism were the order of the day.

'Superb stuff, everyone. So, Dom called this work meeting on The Cocks' behalf to chat about this Chinese Sniffle thingymajig. It seems to have become quite fashionable thanks to a top-secret meeting of our top Johnnie boffins at SAGE.'

Michael Gove looked rattled.

'I must point out that this Sniffle drivel has distracted SAGE from delivering its vitally important findings on the scalding hot coffee issue currently plaguing Whitehall.'

Raab agreed: 'Michael's right. My staff are going down like flies with severe caramel macchiato burns.'

At this, the Defence Bloke stirred and woke up. He announced that the caffeine alert level was now raised to a six, folded his arms, and shut his eyes.

'It seems this Chinese Sniffle might be a taddly bit more problematic than we first thought, Chiefy,' said The Cock, 'and that needs to take priority over macchiato injuries.'

'I fully take that on board, but irrespective of the unfortunate use of the term "problematic", nothing is our fault?' Boris looked worried. Talking about the Sniffle was rather like treading on eggshells or sleeping babies.

'Correct, Chief. The Do Fuck All policy worked a treat, and we can safely deny we knew anything or needed to do something about anything because our heads, quite reasonably, were buried in the sand,' Cummings assured him.

'Excellent,' said Boris. 'Let's have an update then, Matty.'

The Cock consulted his notes. 'Woo-Hoo has been locked down, but luckily flights are pouring in from the rest of China. Let's be honest, we need all the Chinese students we can get to keep our universities going.'

'Damn right. Business as usual, at all times,' bawled Raab, thumping his formica-enhanced table.

'There are over five hundred cases in China and a handful of deaths. Ferguson and his merry boffins have advised me to suspend all direct flights from Woo-Hoo and tell people not to fly to China,' confirmed Boris.

'Ah...OK Chiefy. So, we stopped them coming in some time ago?' asked Gove.

'That's right, direct flights to the UK from WooHoo have been affirmatively suspended,' said The Cock with his customary over-the-top enthusiasm.

'Yes, we know that Matty. Can I ask from when?' questioned Govicus the traitor. The Cock often made him feel vaguely irritated, and today's example of creative obstructionism was no exception.

The Cock re-shuffled his notes.

'Yesterday,' he said cheerfully.

'That's precisely one day before his evil munificence said he was going to lock down WooHoo, the epicentre of this bat Sniffle.' Govicus the traitor almost whispered his words. He felt nervous and didn't want to make it obvious, but it was clear that there had been an outbreak of monumental incompetence somewhere along the line.

Sensing a disturbance in the Do Fuck All force, Boris jumped in.

'Exactly. We've leapt into affirmative action at precisely the right time. This is a stonkingly superb example of British spunk and derring-do.'

Raab banged his table with an ancient silver whelk spoon.

'Let's have three cheers for British spunk!' hooted Boris. 'This reminds me of the time Lord Nelson jumped onto the deck of the San Josef and received the swords of the defeated Spaniards.'

They climbed to their feet, belted out three cheers for British spunk, banged the table with their spoons, and followed it up with a stirring rendition of Jerusalem.

If Cummings appeared oddly distracted, it was because he was processing these facts through his quantum processor-powered mind. 'Let me get this straight, Matty. Woo-Hoo is ground zero of the international Sniffle trade, but we've only just suspended direct flights. However, can I presume that direct flights from other parts of the evil Xi's democratic empire can still come to the UK?'

'Thanks, Dom, yes, that sounds about right,' agreed The Cock.

The cabinet sat in bemused silence, absorbing this viral bomb-shell. Slowly, their inner mental workings transported this infor-mation to various outer regions of their brains. Boris was happy to sit back and let these processes go through their painfully slow motions. It was like asking Moggy to run the London Stock Ex-change with his patented steam-powered internet.

'We do have stragglers, Chiefy.'

'Stragglers, Matty?'

British citizens who couldn't get out of Woo-Hoo in time.'

'We can't leave our wounded on the field of battle. They must be de-straggled.'

'Indeed, Chiefy.'

'Defence bloke, could you kindly scramble some jets and bring our people home. This is our Dunkirk moment.'

Sensing that the defence bloke was otherwise distracted Boris scribbled out an order on a post-it and passed it around the table. On receipt, Priti Patel stuck it to the snoozing ministers forehead.

'I'm pleased to see that we've taken tough affirmative action at Her Majesty's airports to affirmatively keep the Sniffle at bay,' Boris said, breaking the silence.

The Cock raised his hand.

'Boys' room, Matty?' asked Boris

'No, but can I tell everyone what additional measures we've been taking please, Mr Prime Minister?'

'Certainly, if you would be so kind as to illuminate the rest of the cabinet as to what affirmative steps we've taken.'

'In conjunction with the Home Secretary, the UK border force has been instructed to ask people if they have the Sniffle.'

There was a sharp intake of breath from the room.

'That's Jolly draconian stuff, Matty. Are we asking them in Chinese or English?' asked Boris.

'English. We don't want to panic people unnecessarily by having them understand anything. This is an extra layer of security on top of our leaflets.'

'A formidable deterrent that will protect the country for many years to come,' said Boris, proud of his kick-ass team.

'We've also put a new phone number on our leaflets, so they call someone if they start to feel a bit woozy. It diverts to the Keep a Clean Sheet laundrette in Solihull,' said The Cock.

'That's a stonkingly superb touch, Matty, and none of the foreign blighters will be able to ring that number in English because they can't read English and don't know how to use a British mobile phone.'

The Cock nodded excitedly. 'Oh, and I've accidentally pencilled a COBRA in a few days' time. Your attendance is required, Prime Minister, as always.'

'Accidentally?' asked Boris, wondering how The Cock had managed to fill his head with images of a Viking horde ransacking Downing Street.

'Sorry, Chiefy. I was copying and pasting into my digital diary. You know how it is.'

'No, I don't, Matty, but it sounds like you're expecting me to turn up for a meeting that you've called accidentally because you've accidentally pressed a button on your computer.'

Spreadsheet Saj decided now was the perfect opportunity to stick a knife into the health secretary's bollocky regions and twist it around Seppuku style. 'A prime minister can only miss a COBRA in the direst of emergencies, and they cannot be cancelled.'

Cummings rocked back on the legs of his malnourished cockney chair. 'You're technically correct, Spreadsheet, but nothing in the statute book says a prime minister is expected to attend an accidental COBRA.'

There was an audible sigh from Boris. At times like this, Dommers was worth his weight in gold.

'Matty, you know how I am with meetings. Perhaps you could stand in for me? I will be terribly busy celebrating Chinese New Year at Downing Street. They'll be a lion dance and the chance to meet the Chinese ambassador, who is from China and is Chinese, incidentally.'

'We also need to have an affirmative chat on the post-Brexit trade deal front,' said The Truss.

'Thank you, The Truss. That's the real business of the day. There you are, Matty, these are the matters that are occupying the keen political mind, not an irrational panic over some imported Sniffle.'

'Righto, Chiefy,' The Cock replied.

He was bursting with energy. He'd never been PM before, not even a stand-in PM.

'Very well and with that I'll bring the meeting to a close. Ah…now does anyone have any questions?'

The cabinet collectively averted their eyes and coughed into the hands.

'One thing occurred to me,' said Boris.

'Of course, go for it, Chiefy.'

'We have all the equipment to deal with this Sniffle business, don't we, Matty?'

The Cock sat bolt upright. Was this one of the PM' famous blindsiding techniques he'd picked up from Cummings? Boris had already told him to tell everyone that the nation was the best prepared in the whole wide world ever. Perhaps he was testing his mettle.

'Everything anyone could ever ask for. We have to keep people safe, apart from cross-channel riff-raff, of course. I've instructed NHS UK to have a specialist bed and up to ten ordinary beds free across the system in case someone picks up the Sniffle. We've ordered an extra box of bandages from our friends in Indonesia, tons of medical what-nots from Turkey, and a bulk box of household gloves from the Lidl in Romford.'

'Splendid stuff, Matty, it sounds like everything is in hand. Very well, with that, I'll bring the meeting to a close.'

Priti Patel trained a high-powered blowtorch on her untouched pie and mash. Rather than actual food, it seemed to be more in keeping with the sort of thing you'd find on the floor of a portable toilet on the third day of Glastonbury. 'It would be jolly useful to train our border force wallahs in how to identify a bat in case someone tries to smuggle them in.'

'Indeed, PP, a superb point. I have one here expressly for that purpose,' said The Cock.

The Cock pulled a cat box out from underneath his table. The ministers stirred from their somnolent state and gave it their full attention.

'I'd like everyone to meet Monty the bat. He's highly trained and perfectly at home with humans.'

The Cock opened the cage, and all hell broke loose. A small, vicious, flappy object rocketed out of the cage with its Sat Nav programmed to attack Liz Truss's hair. The Truss screamed blue murder.

'Monty. Here's a good boy. Come back to Daddy!' yelled The Cock.

Monty wasn't having any of it. It was mating season in the bat world and The Truss' hairpiece was far more sexually enticing than a cat box full of foul-smelling guano. The Truss reacted quickly. She managed to grab Monty, throw him across the room, and make a break for the door. Far from quelling his ardour, this only served to ratchet up his hormones. He took a deep breath and rocketed after his prey. The rest of the room sat there in contemplative silence, listening to The Truss screams fade down the stairs out onto Dick Van Dyke Road and into the unexplored wilds of the cockney badlands.

Boris looked around the room. 'Golly goodness, one fears that dear old Liz has become a veritable cavewoman.'

Morning
Boris's Bathroom, 11 Downing Street

Boris felt frustrated. The day hadn't exactly started with a rip-snorting whizzbang, what with Young Symonds on the warpath. She had kicked open the door to his bathroom while he was sitting in holy communion with the porcelain gods. They had separate bathrooms as Boris loathed listening to shrieky commercial radio stations while he brushed his teeth. There was a special place in hell for the purveyors of banal ads and hideous repetitive jingles. He'd given clear instructions to the culture secretary to shut the abominations down once he'd finished booting all the anti-government lefties and so-called socialist comedians out of the BBC.

To add a dollop of insult to a plateful of injury, Young Symonds had interrupted his enjoyment of an opinion piece in the *Daily Telegraph* written by one of his old chums. Tobias Smythe-Farquhar-Smythe, the fourth Viscount of Romney, was making the admirable suggestion that working-class types with an excess of tattoos and who wore baseball caps for no discernible reason, should be burned at the stake. It felt radical, right of centre perhaps, but it was the sensible thing to do. With his stonkingly superb world record majority in the house, he had no doubt he could shove it through. He'd decided to run it past Dommers when Princess Nut Nut – as some of the quislings had taken to calling her – shredded the morning's peace and quiet.

'FFS. Seven-thirty in the morning, Boris? Who on earth gets up at that time?'

It was at moments like this when he wondered whether having a baby was the life-affirming, joyous occasion everyone cracked it up to be.

'It's all Matty's fault,' he said defensively, wondering how he could safely avoid the well-documented horrors of the birthing experience. Young Symonds was most insistent that he be present. He'd need to lean on The Truss and see if she could conjure up an international incident of some description. That would mean urgent flights abroad and agreeable five-star accommodation into the bargain. All she needed to do to spark an armed conflict was post a photo of herself on Facebook shaking her fist at some Johnny Foreigner types.

'Of course, it is Bumble. It's always someone else's fault.' She ruffled her hair and launched into a passable imitation of the prime minister. 'I didn't make racist comments, I didn't write shit motoring articles, I didn't squeeze the first lady's thigh, I didn't lie to Her Madge.'

'There's no need for that, Sweetpea,' said Boris, stung by the hurtful barbs. 'The idiot completely buggerated his digital diary and it's a COBRA. They cannot be cancelled. You need to be there. My eyes and ears as it were.'

'But why such an ungodly hour? When you arrange one, it's never before half past ten, like the one back in November when you called a COBRA after the hideous northern plebs left their taps on.'

'This is different. The Cock cocked up his digital diary,' explained Boris.

'I thought you were the prime minister, not that saucer-eyed fanatic who walks around the place with his thumb firmly up his arse.'

'Someone has to be my oculus and auribus, dearest darling.'

'Not at seven-thirty in the morning, they don't. I call half past ten a civilised hour. Only Neanderthals are up and about at seven-thirty to steam clean their knuckles and feed mushy peas to their ragged-trousered little gibbons.'

'I asked him to stand in because I'm entertaining the Chinese ambassador. I'll be expected to join in with the lion dance and do some painting with small children.'

She noticed the twitch in his left hand. A tell-tale sign that his fear of young children, those well-known creatures of unparalleled mayhem, had been triggered.

'Can't you just put on your hard hat and hi-vis vest and drive a bulldozer through brick walls for the day?'

'They'll be plenty of time to explore full turn tipping loads and shovel capacity after Brexit.'

'I still don't see why I should have to sit in on a boring meeting.'

'We all have to make sacrifices, Sweetpea.'

Thinking that would be the end of it, Boris turned back to his newspaper. However, he underestimated Sweetpea's inner rage mechanism. She had other ideas on what personal sacrifice meant, but having to attend a beastly COBRA was not one of them. Before he had time to react, she leaned over behind him, pushed the newspaper in his face and grabbed the remaining roll of Harrods William Morris print, luxury bamboo toilet paper.

'You can't deprive a prime minister of his bamboo toilet paper.'

'Sacrifices must be made, Bumble,' she said and stormed off.

24 January
Reception for the Chinese Ambassador, Downing Street

For the Prime Minister of Britain and its colonies, the universe slowly focused. A mass of stars coalesced into the bricks and mortar of Downing Street. A heavy meal, unsavoury personal hygiene matters, and a bottle of white Burgundy had conspired to form an unexpected cold front of brain fog. Now Boris remembered where the bloody hell he was. A man in an immaculate well-cut suit stood in front of him. He didn't look altogether very British. His hand stretched out, and he seemed to know who Boris was for some inexplicable reason. The chummie seemed to be expecting some kind of response. Fortunately, a translator magically appeared to do Boris's work for him and cut through the guesswork.

'Prime Minister Johnson, may I introduce Xi Lui Xiaoming, the Chinese Ambassador, and his wife, Mrs Xiaoming, the aforementioned wife of the Chinese Ambassador.'

Boris reluctantly shook hands. One of the drawbacks to having a world-beating political career was meeting foreign dignitaries from foreign climes. Minor foreigners such as waiters,[10] ski instructors, and Russian newspaper proprietors were all well and good, but dignitaries, on the whole, were to be despised. After

---

[10] see Gino @ MAMMA MIA's

being officially despised, they would be filed in Lady Hortense's burgeoning UNTRUSTWORTHY filing cabinet. Despite Dom's advanced 'meeting foreigners etiquette classes', he never knew where to stick his hands, for starters, or his tie, for that matter. As per bloody usual, the damn thing had taken the opportunity to slip its moorings in the stiffening breeze and flap around like some giant uncontrollable octopus tentacle. Everything he did teetered on the brink of a third-degree gaffe catastrophe. If it weren't for his hands and tie, it would be his mouth. There was a veritable rogues gallery of prime time 'foot in it' moments. He had no time for all this diplomacy gibberish. All Johnnie Foreigner needed to do was speak up, speak English, and listen to what he had to say. Then, and only then, would everyone get along splendidly.

The Chinese put their tried and tested bowing and scraping routine through its paces while Boris cast an appraising eye over Mrs Chinese Ambassador. He shook her hand with characteristic vim while part of his brain, OK, most of his brain, went into automatic top-totty appraisal mode. He felt there was potential there for a jot of diplomatic thigh squeezing. It would, he conceded, be an audacious move, but someone would have to do it if it meant advancing the old trade deal talks. The risks were obvious, but she did have a certain inviting look in her eye. He'd have to check with Marty and thoroughly review the seating arrangements for the evening banquet.

Mr Xiaoming, the Chinese Ambassador and husband of Mrs Chinese Ambassador, had come to join in with the celebrations for the Chinese New Year at the request of the prime minister himself. He knew it was all a decadent imperialist smokescreen for some small talk about the wonders of Brexit. No doubt it would disintegrate into some unintelligible wibble about global Britain before the usual headlong dash down the rabbit hole of a world-beating trade deal. How a once proud empire conducted itself these days was depressing and predictable.

The British had precious little to offer beyond fridge magnets, designer handbags, Egyptian cotton Marks and Spencer's socks, and potted plants. Yet they persisted in suffering from the nationalistic delusion they had any influence in a world that hated their arrogant, stinking, festering guts. A country incapable of manufacturing its own clothing or cheap, shoddy, made in China, Chinese Christmas decorations, was beyond a joke. Without the might of communist industry and know-how, Christmas in the West would be dead. There would be no tinsel or bumper packs of pointless greetings cards, inflatable Santas or LED lights. That would bring about the end of western civilisation and Christianity, for that matter. Evil Emperor Xi's masterplan for world domination, rubber-stamped by the Chinese People's Democratic Freedom Loving Party, was bang on track.

Lui had been instructed to play along with the British, giving them some cause for optimism. President Xi had told him that one day, the decadent pigs would be their slaves. He said Hong Kong was only the start, and he should know, right? He was the most powerful Evil Emperor on the face of the planet. Forget Trump who was merely a bumbling amateur – much like Boris, his inflatable fanboy – on the world stage.

Mr Chinese Ambassador watched Boris engage in diplomatic small talk with Mrs Chinese Ambassador. These people would happily sell their grandmothers if they thought a trade deal was in the offing. They didn't stand a cat's snowball in hell. Lui thought about this for a few seconds. That didn't sound right. Was it a cat's chance in hell or something to do with snowmen or snowballs? This is what happens when you spend too long in the company of people of such low intelligence as the British. They contaminate the pure party mind. All this Elysian pie-in-the-sky bollocks about personal freedoms and individual liberty, reading whatever you feel like, and the inalienable right to change TV channels with your own remote control. Western civilisation was a drug fuelled, cultural abomination. The people could not be trusted. That was one of the Evil Emperor's favourite sayings. Only the party and its infinite wisdom could wear the crown of trust.

He recalled the terrible incident with Mrs Xiaoming. She'd almost become a victim of Western conversion therapy. That was the result of a deadly British libertarian laissez-faire toxin at work, poisoning her brain. Without realising what she was doing, she had picked up the TV remote and switched channels. Within the blink of an eye, she'd gone from a profoundly fascinating black-and-white documentary on uneducated peasants tilling fields in Henan province to *I'm A Celebrity Get Me Out of Here*. It was a moment of madness but the effect on poor Mrs Xiamong had been immediate and near fatal. She'd been forcibly repatriated, her mind emptied and reprogrammed. They were almost too late. The finest team of Huawei brain surgeons and psychologists had been scrambled after a despicable and depraved Mumford and Sons CD had been found in her carry-on luggage. Only after a full Western detox was she permitted to fly back to the embassy.

Even thinking about it caused the ambassador to break out in a cold sweat. His heart was racing. Seeing Boris in full flow, with his corrupt laissez faire tentacles threatening to deep throat the wife, reminded him that he needed to return to Beijing. There, he could check into rehab and renew his prescription for those extra strength anti-decadence pills. Being in the West for so long was having an adverse effect on his health.

The lion dance ceremony was about to kick off. Boris chatted with some Chinese school children who'd been ferried in from a Chinese school somewhere in London. He found it all awfully confusing.

'I say Raaby, I'm reliably informed that these little foreign blighters attend a Chinese school in London. That's a bloody long way for them to come every day.'

'No, Chiefy. It's a Chinese school in London for Chinese school children who live in London.'

'Ah…so no travelling from the Chinese mainland involved?'

'No, Chiefy.'

'Excellent. Have you had a crack at the old arts and crafts or the pop-up calligraphy class?'

'I had a pootle around at the old calligraphy, Chiefy.'

'Good man. I trust you've mastered it. Needs a jolly steady hand by all accounts.'

'Didn't fare too badly if I say so myself. I can now write "Get Brexit Done" in Chinese.'

Boris was uncomfortably aware of the presence of a small child by his side. The unpleasant little fellow was armed to the teeth with paintbrushes and pots. All no doubt made in the slave labour camps of the Peoples Republic of Inhuman rights. Flecks of foam appeared on the prime ministerial lips. His left hand twitched. Competition time! When it came to self v child in the painting stakes, the self would prevail at all bloody costs. His left hand had upgraded to going like the proverbial clappers. He was up for a battle, and this child would get a damn good thrashing on the field of artistic honour. Ambassador Lui noticed and misunderstood the Boris twitch, rapidly forming the impression that the prime minister was getting down with the groove and had begun the Lion Dance ahead of schedule.

Raab knew the symptoms for what they were. Boris could not suppress his competitive urges. He moved in closer.

'Ah, this young man merely wants you to start the Lion dance, Chiefy. Deep breaths.'

Boris took some deep breaths and calmed. The hand tremors slowed.

'He does? Oh, thank God. Very well, Chinese urchin, please tell me what I need to do. Does it involve rugby tackling unsuspecting children? I'm jolly good at that sort of thing.'

The young boy pointed at four men dressed in traditional Lion Dance costumes, slap in front of Boris.

'Ah, these fiendish oriental Johnnies? I wondered what on earth they were up to.'

'You have to dot their eyes and ears with paint to wake them up,' the boy said and handed Boris the paint pot and brush. The prime minister reciprocated with a low bow.

'Let's see if the Big White Chief can teach you heathens a thing or two.'

Boris dutifully painted the lions. They pretended to wake up and performed a dance sequence, accompanied by a tuneless dirge of drums and insanity inducing cymbal dingy-dinging. Boris attempted to get down with the groove and rocked up and down on his highly polished business brogues. The dance lessons he'd had with Theresa May since she'd set the African continent alight with her prowess on the dance floor had most certainly paid dividends. The throng of Chinese people packing out Downing Street were mesmerised. They smiled appreciatively, took photographs, and pointed excitedly at his slick dance moves.

Ambassador Lui jotted down notes and Mrs Ambassador recorded a video for the benefit of the Glorious People's Democratic Revolutionary Party's secret services. The British Prime Minister had caught him on the hop. They'd seen the top-secret video of him dancing at an Xmas party with a woman wielding a light sabre, but this was on another level. For years video evidence and reams of data supported the widespread belief that Boris was little more than a clod-hopping buffoon equipped with two left feet and all the natural rhythm of a beached whale. He was clearly a gifted dancer. Lui wondered how this would go down in Beijing. The Evil Emperor thought he had all the moves, but Boris was in a different league altogether.

Something made Ambassador Lui look up. Cutting a swathe of bright red Burberry through the crowd came a freshly de-bat-ted and Monty-free Liz Truss. She was headed straight towards him. There was a glossy brochure tucked under her arm. The dastardly British had outsmarted him. They'd changed their normal negotiating processes. The colonial bastards had jumped straight from small talk to a trade deal. That meant a lightning-fast blitz of Liz bloody Truss, a woman with less personality than a crushed Styrofoam cup. He looked around frantically for an escape route. There was no escape. He could see Boris grinning at him like a guilty schoolboy. Raab and his security men were to his left; the crowd of children to his right. The British had beaten him at his own game. He was completely boxed in. Truss moved in for the kill. She came up close and waved her brochure, clipboard, and biro in his face. He quickly calculated that the only way out of this trap would be to put his signature on a tragically disadvantageous fridge magnet deal.

31 January, Brexit Day
Downing Street

Boris was up extra-jolly-especially early. Aside from the day he would be crowned King of the World, this would be the most fantastic day of his life, the pinnacle of a glorious career, and what he'd been working towards. Thanks to the tireless work of all those Euro-sceptics who had staged mass protests against the introduction of the croissant to Britain, the land of sunny pastures and green uplands was right here, right now – on our bloody doorstep.

He'd been up all night, thinking about the staggering enormity of it all. Writing the world's finest motoring articles, picking up parking tickets like confetti, and somehow finding the time to offend ninety-five per cent of the English-speaking world seemed to belong in the dim and distant past. 'Bring in Brexit, and you'll be bigger than Churchill and a bona fide national hero,' Dom told him during the interview process. Freedom from the vindictive and petty-minded EU was the only thing that counted, and here it most jolly well was, even though he hadn't, at times, fully believed in it.

He strode into the bedroom and threw open a pair of £1573.46 per metre Yamamoto designer curtains in a matt indigo colourway.

'Arise, Young Symonds, the most glorious day in British history is upon us.'

'Oh, do fuck off, Boris, it's way too early,' said Young Symonds from the depths of her hand-stitched couture quilt.[11]

'Freedom doth beckon, oh dearest one.'

'It's eight-twenty whatever, and I've got a stonking hangover.'

'I can deploy my patented tried and trusted anti-woozy cure for early morning hurty heads.'

'Getting Dom to throw a bucket of cold water over me would be an engagement cancelling, ring jammed six inches deep in your forehead, kind of event.'

---

[11] Assume Yamamoto again unless advised to the contrary.

'Roger on that, your loveliness. I'll pop down and see what the dear boy is up to.'

'Humping the bloody furniture at a guess,' groaned Young Symonds, pulling a pillow[12] over her head.

Boris bounded down the staircase whistling Rule Brittania. He marched along the hallway, only pausing to salute the portraits of the few surviving paintings of his predecessors that had survived Young Symonds' Downing Street art coup d'etat. She'd buried most of them behind her Banksy's, posters of Campbell's soup cans, and a pickled shark in a tank she'd affectionately called 'Raaby.' It was evident that the dear girl had a troubled mind. He reflected that he might have to consider a matrimonial trade-in if the quality of the artwork deteriorated any further. The situation certainly needed to be closely monitored.

He found Dom in splendid Anti-Christ mode, suspended six feet off the ground, lounging on Young Symonds' bright pink Yamamoto eco-designer sofa. The dreadful, working-class, builder types were engaged in lowering it down through the roof in anticipation of Boris's imminent resignation and move out of Downing Street.

'Morning, Chief.'

'Ah, Dommers. Top of the morning, and what a fantastic morning it is.'

'Why's that then, Chief?'

'Brexit day, of course. The biggest day of our lives – vive La Brexit.'

'Not mine, Chief.'

---

12 See previous Yamamoto footnote.

'What do you mean, not yours? Surely the tremendous achievement of Getting Brexit Done leaves everything else gathering dust at the bottom of a cocked hat?'

'Come into the stateroom, and I'll show you what I mean.'

Intrigued, Boris followed his chief senior special adviser as he pushed through a door. It took a few seconds for his eyes to become accustomed to the darkness. The room erupted with thumping music and disconcerting flashes of neon lighting. Young Symonds came out of nowhere to throw her arms around his neck. Mrs McVey, dressed like a cocktail waitress and speaking fluent Scouse, which no one else understood, offered him a glass of Prossey on a silver tray. Through the gloom, he made out the outlines of various cabinet ministers dancing the morning away. Govicus the traitor was by himself in the corner, making weird nineties-style rave shapes, giving the impression of a paralytic octopus on stilts.

'What do you think, Chief?'

'Govicus? An absolute basket case. Surely you won't be shoehorning him in when I've evacuated the premises?'

'Not Govicus, Chief, it's your Brexit day celebration.'

'Corking, Dommers.'

'I thought it would be a good preparation for tonight's Brexit party celebration.'

'The entire country will be rejoicing. The internet will explode, they'll be street parties across the land with bunting and union jack flags hung from every pub window. My last day as PM. A glorious day we'll never forget.'

The Truss materialised at Boris's side. She looked like she had something on her mind, a look that suggested a glorious day wouldn't ever enter The Truss equation. EVER! The problem with dearest Liz, thought Boris, was that the woman never switched off, being physically incapable of separating work from reality. Non-work time never registered with The Truss.

'Chiefy, we need to sit down and discuss the finer points of the fridge magnet, Cornish pasty, and potted plant deal,' she said.

Boris wagged a finger in protest.

'It's a party, Liz.'

'I know that, but we must go through the refund policy with a fine toothbrush.'

'A fine toothbrush?' He was normally eager to point out her eccentric use of malaprops, but this afternoon, he couldn't be arsed. Brexit day was all about shotting down multiple glasses of Prossey. He decided to be pleasant. Exude civility. Young Symonds would be proud. He was being a bit grown up at last.

'I feel sure it can wait, Liz. Prossey?' He gestured towards Mrs McVey.

'Not while I'm on duty, Chiefy.'

'Please, Liz, take it from me, have the day off, just for today.'

From across the room, Cummings' eagle eyes spotted the clear and imminent threat to the Chief's relaxation time. He nodded to Marty, and The Truss found herself being held up by her shoulders and escorted out of harm's way by several burly members of the security team. By the time his chief senior, special adviser returned, Boris was grooving away to 'Dancing Queen' with Young Symonds, thanks to Dom requesting the presence of Mrs

MacNamara, the studious Keeper of the Karaoke Machine, a certifiably dull woman who ran the pencil sharpening department in Whitehall.

'You should now have a complete Truss-free day, Chief.'

'Thanks, Dommers. What have you done with her?'

'No need to worry, Chief. I had security chain her to Churchill's writing desk. We now have a Truss-free, Sniffle-free zone until we catch the Brexit express.'

'Stonkingly superb stuff, Dom. The Brexit express?'

'The train, Chief. Cabinet away day at the National Glass Blowing Centre in Sunderland. The great engines of government are temporarily relocating.'

'It sounds utterly ghastly.'

'It's all part of levelling up.'

'Can I at least polish off my prossey? I need something to maintain my bouncy tone if I'm heading off to the unpleasantness of the northern Badlands.'

'Indeed, Chief. You have half an hour, then it's full steam ahead.'

Later That Evening
Downing Street Reception Area

Three quarters squiffed and a little unsteady on his feet after surviving a gruelling afternoon of glassblowing, Boris banged a large gong with vim and a degree of awkward abandon. He found himself being stared down by a merry bunch of surly Downing Street staffers. They'd been forced to attend a mega event by Cummings on an *'or else'* basis. Frankly, they didn't see the point. For most of them it meant an additional few hours of unpaid slave labour, drinking English sparkling 'wine', listening to half-pissed ministers telling them they loved them and fending off unsolicited advances. The one bit of good news was that Dilyn had finally made himself useful and sunk his teeth into Spreadsheet Saj's leg. Following a fanfare from the household flugelhorn blowers and undaunted by the sight of blood, Boris thumped a table and launched into a speech extolling the virtues of Brexit, the greatest moment in British history.

His captive audience reluctantly applauded, desperate for him to finish so they could keep the sheer mindbogglingly tedium to a minimum and fuck off home (FOH). Boris, however, was in no mood for wrapping things up. He was on a roll. He thanked Cummings for coming up with the world-beating epigrams, 'Get Brexit Done', 'Take back Control and 'I'd like a Divorce, Please.' He rabbited on about colossal building projects, the nation returning to pounds, shillings, and pence, safer streets, and reducing the BBC back to one channel and all in black and white, thanks very much. Furthermore, the Tory giftshop was open for business. As a reward for their hard work staffers could take full advantage of a whopping five per cent discount on memorabilia such as Boris mugs, Boris tea towels, and Boris oven-ready oven gloves.

Boris was oblivious to the fact that people would rather have nails banged into their foreheads than listen to his drivel. Naturally, he was convinced he'd struck all the right emotional chords. Once his speech was over, everyone was frogmarched up the rear staircase to join him and Young Symonds on the roof of number ten. To the badly recorded BONGS of Big Ben and a frenetic burst of techno music, they had a grandstand view of Jacob Rees-Mogg, ably abetted by Mrs McVey, light the fuse to a single Standard made in China fireworks rocket. The device, a first for British ingenuity and design, shot up precisely forty-three feet before fizzling out and dropping back to earth where it crash landed on Boris's left foot.

Young Symonds enjoyed the sight of a Bumble in pain but wished she'd been more insistent about attending the Brexit party in Parliament Square where chivalrous Mr Farage had installed a huge steam powered Gloat machine. Instead, they had to settle for watching a small TV screen with a live feed from Dover listening to the tortuous national anthem as a three-hundred-foot-high image of Boris sticking two fingers up to the French was projected on to the White Cliffs.

Brexit was done. Accompanied by wild cheering from Rees-Mogg and McVey, and muted applause from the staffers, Boris was a free man once again. Young Symonds could now begin the process of steaming the gold wallpaper off the walls and they could make good their escape. HUZZAH!

February 2020

1 February
Downing Street

Cummings lay sprawled out on Young Symonds' new pink sofa. Here it was, in all its gaudy zebra-striped glory, ready to be shipped out. It may be the latest thing in eco-sofa design, but it wasn't as comfortable as the ancient tatty John Lewis sofa Mrs May had left behind. Boris had customised it with a few glasses of white burgundy to give it an authentic lived-in feel. That was a sofa a chap could comfortably sink into and let his thoughts drift away from the constant noise of plotting and scheming. In its well-worn and threadbare embrace, he could contemplate the congenital defects of ministerial muppets and work on his re-design of political thinking from the ground up.

It was rare indeed that a piece of furniture could provide such an excellent base for mansplaining female underlings and illicit cigar smoking. Suitably relaxed, his brain would go into hypersonic blue-sky mode, spaffing out all manner of ideas and 'jump across the tracks to open the kimono and make a paradigm shift into feng shui, watsu thinking'. This new object d'scorn, on the other hand, was tailor-made for delivering blunt force trauma to the rib cage and/or giving you arse grapes if you sat in one position for more than three minutes. It was a clear case of style over substance. That rather summed up Young Symonds in a nutshell.

It had taken him a dog's age to make himself comfortable on something more suited to moonlighting as a gruesome exhibit at the London Dungeon. He'd adjusted his pile of newspapers and moved the marble-topped side table with his mug of steaming black coffee eleven times since arriving.

For some reason manipulating the feng shui, watsu chakras into their correct alignment was proving troublesome, even after a fresh battalion of AA batteries in the laser protractor. He noticed a few spilt drops of coffee but nothing that would cause offence. He hunched over the table and mopped up the offending liquid with a DC monogrammed shirt sleeve. Then came the ceremonial opening of a box of chocolate truffles from Great Aunt Morpeth he'd managed to squirrel away since Christmas. He sat back and stared up at the ornate plaster ceiling moulding. The builders would return tomorrow to replace the unsightly holes in three floors. That added around £75,000 to the refurb bill. The best part of £200,000 and now they were doing a runner with whatever they could take with them. He wasn't bothered who the party grandees brought in next. They all hated him. As long as the next man (he could predict with 100% accuracy that it wouldn't be a woman – not after Mrs May) was suitably gullible, easily manipulated and controllable, that was fine by him.

Finally, he scanned the morning's headlines after making himself cosy and vaguely Bohemian. There were pictures of Boris saying 'Get Brexit Done' for the 5,673rd time, some vital tittle-tattle about Meghan's new handbag, and an in-depth survey in the *Mail* reporting that rich people tend to have more money than poor people.

Cummings swivelled a beady eye to the grandfather clock. Ten twenty-seven. Still time before the grandees arose from their coffins in Tory HQ. It wasn't every day he had the opportunity to grind up a batch of his favourite and finest Arabica coffee beans. These were an exquisite find. Roasted in a yurt on the foothills of the Andes and sustainably sourced. He savoured the word 'sustainability' almost as much as the coffee. It was one of the first words he'd introduced after he'd made it look as though Boris had brought him into Downing Street. The best thing about it was that it didn't mean anything. Sustainability was, after all, doublethink for eco-friendly bollockology.

'Morning, Dommers,' rumbled a blurry, hurty-head Boris. He dragged himself and his freshly packed cabin case into the room and sat beside Cummings. A large cumulus cloud of wooziness was the order of the day, but it was merely the price to be paid for what, if his patchy recollections were anything to go by, had been a stonking corker of an evening. He couldn't recall any cabinet drinking games, but it must have been a good night. He had a warm, glowing feeling after the Brexit celebration.

His speech had gone down brilliantly and when his eyes opened, he'd watched the sunlight cascade through the new Yamamoto rattan shutters. He visualised a new, glorious, British nirvana, a kingdom uncluttered by the bureaucratic pen-pushing jimbo-wimbo of foreign johnnies who were massively jealous of everything we had in this brilliant country of ours. Without a doubt, he'd woken to the pumping economic piston of a bright new dawn. The UK was back under control. We will conquer the world with our trade deals. We will be stonkingly superb Global Britain.

He soon spotted Dom slouching in classic barefoot Dommish style on Young Symonds' sofa.

'Morning Chief. Bang on time.'

'I am?'

'Our meeting with the grandees.'

'Heavens above, I'd completely forgotten. My sign off meeting.'

The woozy clouds evaporated.

'What ho, chaps,' growled a basso profondo voice from the doorway. An icy wind whipped through the room. Boris and Cummings shivered. It heralded the arrival of the Tory living dead: the grandees, Sir Bob and Lord Philip. These were the influential powerbrokers who had set the political bearings of the party for decades. They were the only people Boris and Cummings respected and, more importantly, feared. With a single look, they could tear out your soul at a thousand paces and leave it flopping about, impaled on the Downing Street railings. It was like being summoned before Emperor Palatine, knowing that the odds were generally stacked in favour of a total skull crushing.

'Job well done,' growled Sir Bob as he took a sip of Arabica's finest.

'The greatest day in the history of our illustrious party,' phlegmed up Lord Philip. He poured a shot of brandy into his coffee.

'We need to talk about the succession, young Master Boris,' said Sir Bob. His eyebrows, which seemed to have an independent life of their own, quivered.

'The thing is, you are surfing a wave of unbridled popularity,' said Lord Philip, who removed a snuffbox from his jacket. 'We have a thunderously large majority and the opportunity to do what we want.'

'Keep the poor poorer, stop spending money on fripperies such as the NHS, invade France and take back the lands seized by Henry the Fifth,' said Sir Bob, rubbing his hands.

Lord Philip took a deep hit off his snuff and sneezed prodigiously. The noise was deafening, like being woken up by a stun grenade. He packed away his snuffbox and leaned across the table. 'Apart from anything else, Boris my lad, our donors are pouring fistfuls of cash into the coffers like there's no tomorrow.'

'Fistfuls,' agreed Sir Bob. 'No tomorrow.'

'Don't you have someone lined up?' asked Boris nervously.

'He's undergoing bible training. Won't be the finished article for a few months yet. Wet behind the ears and all that.'

'Bible training?' Cummings wasn't sure where this was heading.

'Yes, you know, the Tory bible,' confided Lord Philip.

'Britannia Unchained,' said Sir Bob. 'The new boy needs to have a thorough grounding in the Tory commandments,' he explained. 'Thou shalt blame migrants for everything, thou shalt lower taxes for the rich, and thou shalt stop the parasitic working classes from buying more than two packets of digestives at a time.'

'We must bring back the Dickensian workhouse and throw regulations and employee rights onto the bonfire. After that, we support turbo-charged capitalism and abolish high taxes,' said Lord Philip with his trademark libertarian zeal.

'But you promised me my freedom. Young Symonds has already ordered an industrial-strength steamer to remove the gold wallpaper.'

Lord Philip stood and slapped Boris on the back.

'It's all about legacy, Young Master Boris. Legacy. Imagine being the greatest PM the country has ever had, the Churchill of his generation. You'll earn a fortune.'

Damage done, the icy blast preceded them through the door, and the grandees departed to their coffins in the vaults below Tory HQ. Their visitation left Boris with a maelstrom of thoughts to contend with, and the return of his zoinkingly bad hangover. He lifted his coffee but badly miscalculated the angle. Hot black liquid cascaded across the table. *The Daily Mail* took the full brunt of the downpour. The coffee soaked right through it and onto the retina-scorching fabric of the bright pink sofa. He gawped in horror.

'Fuck!' He spotted a smudge of chocolate truffle mixed in with an ever-expanding coffee stain.

'Double, triple and quadruple fuck, Chief.'

Fortunately, Cummings caught sight of Larry the Cat prowling around in the hallway. Before Larry had time to react and engage his ninja-like reflexes, he found himself being roughly manhandled and rubbed vigorously into Young Symonds' vulgar sofa. There was no time to think. His legs were held tight, his claws rendered useless. His assailant had thought of everything.

Cummings hoisted Larry off the sofa and inspected his handiwork. The coffee and fragments of chocolate truffle had transferred rather nicely to the feline's fur.

'All sorted, Chief.'

'Excellent work. Say what you like, but Mr Yamamoto's £2457.05 per square metre hand-painted zebra patterned fabric made a damn good job of resisting astringent liquids,' said Boris, somewhat relieved. 'What shall we do with him?' he said, gesturing to Larry.

'The bins.'

Cummings didn't feel the slightest pang of remorse despite his spiritual kinship with the cat kingdom. He kept a tight grip on Larry, took him out of the stateroom through a side door, and dumped him in a hessian sack beside the bins. Larry hissed and clawed like a deranged demon, but there was no way out. Cummings contemplated the wriggling sack, taken aback by the intensity of Larry's feline violence. He couldn't just leave him there. It would soon attract someone's attention, and before you knew it, the cat would literally be out of the sodding bag.

There had to be a better solution. He heard an engine revving and a screeching of brakes. Without further encouragement, he picked up the cat bag and ran into Downing Street. A small van was executing handbrake turns, burning rubber and sending up toxic clouds of smoke. It slid sideways to a stop outside the front door of number ten. Priti Patel wound down the driver's window and yelled, 'Damn the torpedoes', to a gaggle of open-mouthed journalists. The van was a souped-up immigration van with a dropped suspension. It bumped up and down, blasting out Wagner's Rise of the Valkyries from its deafening sound system. Cummings took advantage of the smokescreen, hurried over to the van, opened the rear door, and hurled Larry inside.

A Little Later

Unlike most posho young ladies of her age, Young Symonds liked to be up with the larks. According to her copy of *Debrett's*, eleven o'clock was the optimum time for young ladies to be on their feet and gadding about. Curiously, the larks in question had caused her to rise at the unearthly hour of twenty-five past ten today. She thought this break in her sleeping habits might be something to do with her pregnancy but couldn't be sure. She texty-poo'd Thomasina Smythe-Smith-Smythe for advice on larks, and she received a message saying that these kind of preggo botherations were best left to nursey.

Today was the day she, Bumble, and Dilyn were leaving Downing Street. She'd made a list of all the furnishings and fixtures they needed to take with them, and the underlings had been given strict instructions on how to steam off the gold wallpaper and carefully remove her treasured artwork. She'd thoughtfully provided white gloves for the purpose.

It was funny, but the closer they came to Brexit Day, she knew she'd miss the old place and dearest Bumble secretly loved being PM. More importantly, it also kept him busy and out of her hair. Quite what she was supposed to do with an unkempt yahoo moping around the place all day, she didn't know. After all, he couldn't go back to being Lord Mayor of London, what with all those oversight committees examining the finer points of his bum hairs. What was he going to do with himself? Waste his time writing those dreadful books on Shakespeare that precisely 0.00% of the population would ever read? Fortunately, the baby would be a distraction. She decided to pay a trip to the world's finest designer sofa to cheer herself up.

Downstairs, she took a left turn into stateroom #4. Surprisingly, she found Bumble there, along with the Prince of Nerdville. Young Symonds wasn't impressed by the sight of open-shirted, bare-footed Cummings on her furniture. At least he didn't look comfortable, which was entirely the point of high-end design. It was there to make a statement. Not the Mrs May, John Lewis statement of 'hello, I'm crushingly dull and grey.' No, the Yamamoto was something far more dynamic. It positively screamed, 'Hello, I have a personality; I can change the flow of interior décor and life itself.' Young Symonds found it intoxicating. She only half listened to a three-quarter apoplectic Boris as he ranted on about being betrayed by the grandees, and he would have to stay on as PM for the sake of the country for a while yet. In the grip of a Japanese designer trance, Young Symonds got down on her knees and stroked the sensual plushness of the luxurious fabric. She heard herself muttering, 'Everything is perfectly alright, Bumble, these things happen. We can stay here if you think it best.' Boris and Cummings were forced to avert their eyes as she ran her tongue down one of the tapered wooden legs.

'Such refined elegance,' she purred.

'Indeed,' said Boris and nudged Cummings hard in the ribs.

'I've explained to the chief that the grandees don't want him to go. He is the most popular prime minister in British history, and he doesn't have to worry about money. He can claim everything through expenses.'

'There's no need to worry, dearest Domsey. I'm fine, and besides, what would Bumble do if he didn't have anything to do? I expect my sofa will come back upstairs.'

'One hundred per cent guaranteed. I'll issue instructions to the workshy lower orders.'

'Forthwith,' said Boris.

'Absolutely maximum forthwith,' added Cummings.

Young Symonds let rip with a dazzling smile. She perched on a sofa arm and ran her hands along the adorable plush fabric and along the back of a cushion. She felt something in her hand. That something didn't feel right. THAT something was something that should never be within a 500-mile radius of an exclusive handmade sofa, with timber hewn from a plantation in the Andes foothills. She lifted her hand. There in her fingers was a small, matted clump of hair. It wasn't human hair, this was…Oh, my bloody God!

'BORRRRRRRISSSSSSS!!!'

Young Symonds' scream reverberated through Downing Street and rocked Whitehall to its foundations. It showed up as a 4.7 magnitude seismic event at the US Geological Survey.

It succeeded in one task: to blow the fuzz of Boris's sledgehammer of a hangover into next week. He thought he'd heard someone screaming at the dullest end of his mind – the mismanaged wasteland section. It didn't take him long to triangulate the source – Young Symonds. He successfully deduced that she was incandescent with rage over *something*. *Something* had irked the dear girl as her incandescentness had rendered her utterly incapable of speech. She had turned into such a primal vision of biological hatred that he feared for his continuing existence in this brave new Brexit world. She held up her right hand and shook it with a surprising degree of ferocity. Her eyes blazed, and in their reflection, he saw it. A knot of revolting hairy gunk that closely resembled Custer's scalp at the end of his last stand. Cripes, it was decision time, and his choices were on the unfortunate side of stark:

- Go for sarcasm (eminently risky).
- Try a dose of upbeat wit (eminently likely to find his toothbrush lodged at a game-changing angle down his throat).
- Resort to coaxing out something that sounded sincere and borderline empathetic (an eminently high-risk level strategy due to his rare stabs at empathy generally coming across as fake and unnatural).

After considering all three in a different order and subsequently rejecting all three (due to both an eminent and imminent threat to life), he went with: 'Is Dilyn moulting? It could be that union jack coat we put him in. The dear boy was in it all night. Perhaps it was too hot for him?'

'It's fucking cat hair.'

'Cat hair, Sweetpea?'

'Fucking CAT hair.'

'Are you sure?'

'Try the tasting menu.'

With that, she jammed the revolting hair/chocolate/coffee combination into Boris's mouth.

'I demand a full investigation. If that is Larry's fur, I'm taking the little shit on a work's outing to the canal.'

Boris attempted to mumble a reply, but an unpleasant wodge of cat hair had successfully attached itself to the back of his throat. He'd be coughing up furballs for a month at this rate.

'I want a DNA sample on my desk within the hour, Mr Cummings.'

'Yes, ma'am.'

She stormed off, leaving her IWH to choke on his hideous cat hair delicacy.

3 February
Downing Street

Boris and Cummings emerged from the front door of number ten. This alerted a pair of dozing police officers who leapt into action and pointed them out to the press pack. The journos couldn't believe their luck. Boris was dressed up as the well-known comic book superhero, Superman. Naturally, they blitzed him with a string of impertinent questions:

'Is that right, Superman? Thousands of people who arrived here from Wuhan have escaped, and you don't know where they are?' – *Guardian*

'Superman, is it true the anti-Chinese airport leaflets haven't worked?' – *Times*

'Why has the UK's stockpile of personal protective equipment now dwindled to two boxes of Elastoplast, prime minister superman?' – *Independent*

'Superman, is it true that drunk seagulls are spreading the virus? – *The Sun*

The questions were relentless. At times like this, Boris wished Gavin Williamson's scheme for anti-press trapdoors in Downing Street was proceeding at a faster pace. His brow furrowed in concentration. He thought he heard BBC reporter Laura Kneussberg's shrill voice cutting through the melee, saying something derogatory about wearing his underpants inside out. He decided not to look up and meet her eyes. That would mean answering a question, and Dommers ordered him to refrain from directly engaging with the enemy.

A diminutive Fiat 500 pulled up to the kerb, and transport supremo Grant Schnipps stuck his head out the window.

'What ho chaps, hop aboard.'

Boris and Cummings squeezed inside.

'Where to, chiefy?'

'The Old Naval College,' said Cummings. A Boris elbow caught him in the ribs. The Chief was having problems manuevering in the narrow confines of the Italian shoebox on wheels.

'WTF, Schnipps? A bloody Fiat? Where's my prime ministerial steed, my magnificent Jag?'

'She's in for her annual service and MOT, Chiefy. I blagged this beauty from Mr Rees-Moggs's junior footman to meet your temporary transportational needs.'

'Only one minor snag, Schnippsy.'

'What's that, Mr Cummings?'

'This temporary transportational solution of yours appears to be squashing the PMs balls into his mouth.'

A Bare Modicum of Minutes Later
Inside Schnipps' Bloody Fiat 500

Boris managed to adjust his low-hanging gentleman's appendages before switching a malevolent eye to Schnipps. Dom had deliberately picked a useless crew for his cabinet, and Schnipps was peak useless. He'd read the assessment reports. The man was practically a full-time vegetable. Dom's logic was that a useless cabinet would be easy to manipulate and bend to the Big White Chief's will. Boris pondered over this and allowed his mind to dream up some medieval torture devices for people like Schnipps. Indeed, he successfully improved on the original designs.

Cummings leant into Boris with the air of an arch-conspirator.

'I'm worried about Spreadsheet Saj, Chief.'

This caught Boris's attention, distracting him from the rather pleasant mental image of his transport wallah's grinning head mounted on a large iron spike outside Fiat's Turin HQ.

Cummings breathed heavily. 'We're having something of a tussle with him.'

This is how political powerplays went on in Westminster – a world of hints, suggestions, nudges, winks, and vague promises that amounted to little more than bugger all. They could break even the most experienced politician into tiny fragments of his or herself, leave the remains drowning in a sea of rumour and conjecture, and all without them ever knowing. At times like this, Boris thought, politics became a grand delusion.

'He won't spend any more money, Chief.'

'You chose him, Dom. It's hardly my fault if the recruiting policy should prove to be inadequate. My understanding is that we pay him handsomely to rein in spending. We are still in the throes of austerity, after all. All departments are under-resourced, and long may that continue.'

'You promised to bung a few quid up north to spend on northerners to stop them migrating south.'

Boris had forgotten about this. One of the burdens of running a country was remembering exactly what he promised to whom and when. He rapidly adjusted his blame game approach and opted for a more pragmatic line of questioning.

'He wouldn't haggle?'

'Nothing. Simply folded his arms, waved his red pen, and shook his fat stupid egg head.'

'Well look, by jingo, I'll have a word, Dom. Part of his job description is to wangle. Besides, we can't have cloth cap northern migrants coming down here and desecrating our green and pleasant land.'

Boris could do without all these back-office shenanigans, but for now, he needed to at least show willing on the getting involved front. After the colossal disappointment of being told to stay on by the grandees, he and Young Symonds had hatched a grand plan of dissent. He'd still need to be an absolute legend and hero, but that didn't mean he couldn't be a bit shit at the job. Make slightly worse decisions, obstruct and delay at all times. This was the Do Things a Bit Shit policy in a nutshell. Eventually, the party vampires would see the light and let him leave gracefully.

'Have you been through my speech, the first ever post-Brexit speech by a Post-Brexit, British Prime Minister?'

'I brandished my favourite biro over this morning's finest arabica beans and annotated it at top speed, Chief. Britain, the superman of Europe. Ergo: The Superman outfit.'

'Corking idea. Britain as the Superman of Europe. That's guaranteed to make the Brussels bean counters gag on their pain au chocolat.'

Cummings pulled open the waxed canvas bag nestling between them on the back seat. He handed Boris a pile of crumpled A4 paper.

'Why the naval college, by the way?' asked Boris.

'British sea power and all that, Chief. It's always good to let Johnny Foreigner know who is boss.'

Old Naval College, Greenwich

Fists pumping, Boris marched towards the ornate, baroque art of the painted hall. Halfway there, he realised he could barely read a word of his speech. It was liberally defaced with a rash of Dom's 'adjustments'. These were feng shui, watsu, blue-sky editorial notes in spidery trails of red ink. On closer examination, they appeared to have been made by a certifiable lunatic. He froze. Was Dom out to sabotage him? Was he in cahoots with Spreadsheet Saj? This wasn't the first time it dawned on Boris that the siren lure of Brexit had gone to Dom's head. But Brexit day and the grandees had made all the difference. He had to make an effort of some description. Brexit, he remembered, was supposedly what he lived for. He had personally delivered it and taken it over the line. He might do a slightly shittier job than normal, but that wasn't going to let that stop him from celebrating. Not now. He pumped the air and took to the stage with relish, noticing that there were no party balloons for some odd reason.

The audience was immediately mesmerised by the UK prime minister addressing them while dressed up as a comic superhero. However, a couple of minutes into his speech, Boris sensed that he was losing them. It was also insufferably hot in the outfit. How on earth did Superman manage to stop trains with one arm behind his back, rescue attractive damsels in distress from high buildings, and keep his quiff in place?

It wasn't classic Boris. The buoyant knockabout, clown about town, had been replaced by a stumbling portly buffoon who didn't seem to want to be there. Out of desperation, he clumsily changed out of the Superman outfit and into a grey suit with matching Clark Kent style glasses.

'Britain,' he said, 'was ready to be the Superman of the world, the defender of our civil liberties and freedoms to ignore any kind of Chinese Sniffle irrationalities that might tempt people into raising the trade drawbridges and prevent the import of fridge magnets. Free, unshackled movement of goods was all part of the divine plan, and who are we to argue with that?'

This was met with a smattering of lukewarm applause.

'Ah, righty ho – now do we have any questions?'

A man stood up in the third row. He wasn't wearing a tie, so it was safe to assume he was a rabble-rousing leftie tosser. Boris steeled himself.

'You said you wanted Britain to be Superman, Prime Minister, but now you've become Clark Kent. Isn't that a reverse phone box manoeuvre – a metaphor for global Britain going backwards to simply Britain?'

Boris was confused. Where were Rees-Mogg and his battalion of bamboo-wielding police officers to enforce some much-needed discipline? There was nothing in his speech about reversals and going backwards. It went against the natural order of things. Something had gone wrong somewhere. He waved his arms and punched the air anyway, then tried to check his speech. The Marxist was thanked for his question, a time-honoured trick for buying precious thinking time. The best course of action was to implement the tried and tested answer the question without answering a question strategy. That was one where Dom's intensive question evasion course for cabinet ministers and prime ministers came in especially handy.

'What I would say in reply is that even when other, far inferior countries feel like closing their borders over this Chinese Sniffle, Britain will run into a phone box like Superman, with our capes flowing and keep the trading beaches open. We are going to stand and fight, rather like that Mayor chappie in *Jaws*.'

Boris wasn't the only confused person in the hall. People looked at each other. Surely it was Clark Kent who ran into a phone box? The Big White Chief's exemplary thinking on his feet skills had deserted him in his hour of need. His metaphors had crumbled, and his thoughts wandered off to Mustique. There they floated around in an idyllic fug of white sandy beaches, bottles of white burgundy, and generously proportioned safari suits. What he wouldn't give to be back there now – swimming in a palm-shaped pool, rugby tackling the Mustique under twelves during a bitterly contested game of quoits or lounging about on a secret beach with Young Symonds.

Another voice brought him crashing down to earth. Boris shielded his eyes. Ye Gods above, it was a woman. Even worse, this one looked like a businesswoman, and they always spelt trouble in his experience. To a man, none of them wore a tie and would likely have a silver dancing pole hidden up their blousey sleeves and want extensive funding for foreign trade missions. This harridan undoubtedly had a Satanic upbringing.

Her question dripped with condescension: 'What you are saying, Mr Johnson, is that if a great white shark turned up at Heathrow, you would merely give it one of Mr Hancock's virus-repellent leaflets?'

'Ah, um, no. We most certainly wouldn't do that. As an environmentally conscious and indeed, a world leader on climate change, feeding sharks with leaflets might be counterproductive.'

'Then you'd keep the beaches open?'

Boris beamed. He was on firmer ground at last. He'd put paid to this devilish female in short order.

'Absolutely. Circling and with its fin sticking out of the water. We are not the labour party who would, without doubt, send the mighty beast for therapy and deduce it has special needs' said Boris, pleased with his skills of political riposte. Not for nothing was he known as the D'Artagnan of political debate at Eton.

'Even if the fish decided to eat some people?' asked the woman. FFS, this springy-haired harpy was nothing if not tenacious.

'There is always collateral damage and piles of bodies, but come what may, this glorious high-octane nation of ours will remain open for business. Brexit will put us back on the roadmap to prosperity, free from the manacles and tyranny of the EU.'

With that, he turned his back and exited stage left. He had no doubt that he'd pulled off a snortingly good speech despite Dom's best attempts to sabotage it.

One Week Later
PM's Study, 11 Downing Street

Boris waltzed in with a pair of strategic 'look busy' files tucked under his arm. The Cock followed close behind with an espresso macchiato and a plate of assorted croissants. Boris cleared a heap of papers off his desk and Hancock noticed a disquieting newspaper headline from the week before. It could hardly have been worse:

IS BORIS SUPERMAN OR A COMPLETE KENT?

The Cock thought it best to ignore the headline and try to think of something else to talk about. On the wall behind the desk were glossy photo's of the current cabinet ministers. Several had darts sticking in them. In Spreadsheet Saj's case there was one right between his eyes. Boris followed his health secretary's uneasy gaze.

'Octavian is clearing out all the Remainer deadwood so he can see the trees, Matty. Major re-kerfuffle going on today,' he said with the air of a Roman emperor.

'Octavian, Chief?' asked Hancock.

'More commonly known as Caesar Augustus.'

'Ah, didn't his wife poison him?'

'Yes, shortly after he ordered civilisation's first cabinet re-ker-fuffle.'

'I'll be damned. That's a ripcorker of an idea, Chiefy.'

'I'm giving all those dozy closet friends with the EU their marching orders and bringing in some replacements who gave their unambiguous support for Brexit.'

'I think you'll find it's called a reshuffle, by the way, Chiefy.'

Boris consulted his notes. He held them up and span them around to show 'The Cock.' Much like the naval college speech, they were graffitied with Dom's spidery scrawl.

'It jolly well looks like "re-kerfuffle". Let me ask you some-thing, Matty. Do you ever have a problem reading Dom's notes?'

'I have to be constantly on my wits, Chiefy. I had to send the last lot to Home Office forensics. Thanks to Mr Cummings, I told the house that we were bringing in new regulations to force people infected with the Sniffle to self-inflate themselves.'

'Why, in the name of King Solomon's Jacuzzis did you tell people to self-inflate? They're not car tyres, or balloons for that matter,' asked Boris after polishing off an almond croissant. Four croissants in under ninety seconds had to be a world record. He'd get Raaby to chuck a Whatsapp over to Macron. The French would be beyond livid.

'That's my point, Chiefy. It was Cummings. That's what it looked like on his sheets. Self-inflate, rather than self-isolate.'

Boris's left hand shook imperceptibly.

'Did anyone notice?'

'Starmer raised a quizzical eyebrow, but I distracted him by referring to him as Mr Stammer. I think I got away with it, no thanks to Dom's red pen.'

'I have some nagging doubts about Dom. He ballsed up my speech at Greenwich and told me it was a ploy to keep the old thinking-on-my-feet skills on their toes. His instructions were to fly by wire and deliver my speeches extempore.'

'Surely not, Chiefy, he's your right-hand man.'

'I had to resort to the trusty dartboard. It was the only way I could make decisions. The Acme patented electronic executive decision-maker circuits are completely burnt out. I might have to raid our Cayman Islands tax base to raise funds for a replacement. In fairness, Dom suggested using an Alexa device and it worked out stonkingly well.'

'An exquisite plan, sir. I admire your reserves of dash and bravado. The anti-no-deal Brexit dimwits need to learn to damn well toe the line in the sand.'

'Absolutely, Matty. I couldn't have put it better myself. I can only have ministers who will do what I say without question and happily sign a letter of blind allegiance when their families are threatened.'

'So…you know, who is…ah…on their way out?'

'That woman with the grating Scouse accent, for starters,' said Boris, barely concealing his contempt for Mrs McVey. 'Spreadsheet Saj as well of course. Look at the dartboard. One of my best shots. Right between the eyes. Besides, he's already pre-empted me by threatening resignation over that unpleasantness with his SPADS.'

'Isn't that a slightly risky, Chief? I thought he was the only person we have who can do the sums,' said The Cock with a massive dose of trepidation.

'So he is, but the grandees have found someone else who can do the sums and lots of them. I'm told he has an extensive collection of calculators. Besides, sums aren't exactly important. If they were, Aristotle would most certainly have a GCSE in maths.

'And will you be retaining the services of the traitor, Brutus Govicus?'

'Old saucepot five-in-a-bed? Indeed, I've wanted to give him the boot for some time, but Alexa assured me that keeping my enemies close was the preferred option. Nothing wrong with betrayal of course, it's an integral part of the game.'

'Do you think they'll be upset when they see their pictures with a dart sticking in them?

'I'll butter them up over a lavish dinner, quiz them about their connections and Schopenhauer's theory of the double-breasted jacket. By the time I've finished with them they'll want to sack themselves. It's a re-kerfuffle tradition, and besides, Mr Williamson has finally furnished me with an emergency trapdoor lever should things turn a taddly bit ugly.'

The PM's Weekly Meeting with Her Madge
Buckingham Palace

If there was one thing the nonagenarian Queen of England and parts of Saffron Walden hated, it was the sight of a grown man wetting himself in throne room #5. She took a long hit off her vape while senior footman #13 tied the laces of her purple Doc Martens.

'FFS Boris, pull yourself together man,' she said, blowing out a plume of noxious fumes.

A small, unplanned leakage from little Boris suggested that big Boris was uncharacteristically nervous. He felt like this before every weekly meeting. It started when Her Madge reduced him to a flatulent bowl of shredded nerves after he told her porkies about the prorogation of parliament the previous year. She'd misheard 'prorogation' as 'copulation', and all hell broke loose. His copy book was irredeemably blotted, despite an agreeable weekend break at Balmoral. Her Madge had driven him and Young Symonds at top speed through the Royal estate in her Land Rover, screeching around the bends while Philip took potshots at the ground staff. There was something unnerving about her commanding presence that reminded him of his first encounter with

Lady Hortense when she nabbed him on his inaugural midnight tuck shop raid at Eton.

Her Madge stomped past Boris, making her regal progress towards throne #6.

'Walk with me, Young Master Boris.'

'Of course, ma'am.'

'Johnson, we have a country to run, and I can't do it by myself.'

Her Madge took her place on the throne, hunched over a solid gold Faberge laptop and punched the ivory keys. Her fingers were nothing if not sprightly.

'No, ma'am, absolutely not, ma'am.'

'Now what's all this my people tell me about our low-life socialist Marxists tricking the idiot Hancock into revealing that Her Majesty's government has plans to deal with the Sniffle.'

'It appears to be true, ma'am. We believe Her Majesty's piss-poor opposition had help from the Russians.'

'Plans? You're not supposed to have plans. Under the Callaghan Protocol of—'

'Nineteen seventy-eight. Yes, I know, ma'am, but they've managed it somehow. Our world-beating boffin wallahs didn't think they could develop such advanced technology that would pull the wool over The Cocks' eyes.'

'Don't get me started on our boffin wallahs, Johnson. They've still not reported back on the Whitehall coffee issue.'

'Apologies, ma'am, but the Sniffle—'

She didn't let him finish. 'They were diverted from their task, Prime Minister. A task that, as you know, has consequences for the palace. Many of our royal staff are outsourced from White-hall, and we have experienced dire consequences of the peasantry drinking coffee at the temperature of molten lava. Especially in the stables.'

'Indeed, ma'am. We strongly believe that technology will provide an answer.'

Her Majesty waved away his excuses.

'I also hear we have a little problem with some boat of ours in the heathen republic of Japan.'

'The *Diamond Princess*, ma'am. She's marooned in Yokohama harbour.'

'Full of this bloody hideous Chinese Sniffle and even more bloody hideous cruise ship passengers, I'm led to believe.'

'Yes, ma'am. We've had our first British death from the virus onboard.'

'Is the boat one of ours?'

'Correct, ma'am. There are more British passengers on board.'

Her Madge raised a regal eyebrow.

'Dead or alive?'

'Alive, ma'am. Mr Schnipps is organising a flotilla of aeroplanes to bring them back home and slap them in quarantine. But we would appreciate some assistance in solving the dilemma.'

'At great expense to the public purse, I daresay, Young Master Boris. I can never fathom why the lower orders are permitted to leave the country, travel on aeroplanes, and disport themselves in a most unseemly fashion overseas. I blame budget air travel. Is the new chancellor aware of these costly extravagances?'

'Of course, ma'am.

'That's some good news at least. Here's One's deal. You transfer One's usual twenty-five per cent to the sovereign grant, and One shall forward the coordinates of this deplorable cruise vessel to RAF high command. This time tomorrow, the only sign of that abominable boat will be boxes of complimentary toiletries and tacky souvenirs floating in Yokohama harbour. Consider your problem dealt with.'

'Thank you, Your Majesty, obliged as always,' said Boris, firmly steering a course to the safe harbour of deferential. It was always jolly tally ho when someone else sorted out your problems.

Her Madge stared at him over the top of her spectacles.

'Are you still here, Young Master Boris? I think it's time you learned to judge when it was time to bugger off. That vicar's daughter, Theresa Wotsit, God rest her soul, had it down to a fine art.'

'Indeed, ma'am.'

The Prime Minister of Britain's green and pleasant land bowed and stepped backwards out of the throne room without attempting to correct Her Madge's view on Mrs May.

'One more thing,' she said as he almost disappeared from view. Her Madge cocked her head to one side, the better to see him over a solid gold teacup, a gift from her dear friend, the Maharajah of Udaipur.

'Yes, ma'am.'

'I feel it might be to your advantage for you and that cock fellow to visit the British PPE stockpile.'

'We have a stockpile of philosophy, politics, and economics, ma'am?

'Personal Protective Equipment, Young Master Boris.'

'Would there be a pressing reason as to why, ma'am?'

'One's servants helped themselves to several tons of it yesterday and have informed One that thanks to your party's infernal austerity measures, stocks are, shall we say, dwindling. If the Sniffle becomes a pandemic, we're going to need more than five boxes of The Cocks' made in bloody China plasters.'

'Yes indeed, ma'am.'

'Yes indeed, Young Master Boris.'

13 February
Fucking off to Chevening

For the rest of February, Boris decided to unplug himself from the government mainframe and set all internal controls to automatic pilot. He urgently needed to put his feet up after ordering six cabinet ministers to be incinerated in a Holloway chicken shop for inappropriate Brexit sentiments, during his re-kerfuffle. He'd also asked The Cock to chair all future COBRA meetings as he was far too busy to pop along. After all, he and Young Symonds had a new holibob to look forward to, and he had some awkward family business to deal with. This was a week or two down at Chevening with its boating lakes, fiendishly tricky maze, and luxurious Downton Abbeyesque epicness. It was, he thought contentedly, the perfect hideaway from the stresses and strains of high political office and more importantly, the press Johnnies wouldn't be able to ask any idiotic questions.

Chevening House

Boris's life as Prime Minister had disintegrated into a seemingly endless stream of bloody 'ands'. There were too many 'ands' in his life for his liking. Every day was an 'and' day. It was simply too much.

Chevening was, as he gazed reflectively out the windows at the pouring rain, a safe retreat from Storm Tosser, a violent weather conflagration that had left most of the country under six feet of contaminated sewage water.

He ordered staff not to send him any departmental jibber jabber to his red box. Dom had instructed that all correspondence, including emails, must be printed on A4 paper and could not be more than 125 characters long, due to austerity measures, if they wanted the PM to read it. Reading would only take place on Tuesday afternoons, following a glass or two of 2009 Chateau Mouton Rothschild Pauillac Premier Cru from the extensive cellars.

There was no chance of him reading anything at weekends. Weekend working was strictly for the birds. The compulsory opening of his own post since returning from Musty was driving him bonkers and he needed to keep an eye out for a few minor things. As recommended by Her Madge he'd recently visited the UK stockpile of Personal Protective Equipment with The Cock. For centuries, it had been stored in the cellar of the Nelsons Arms public house on the Old Kent Road. There was plenty of it to go around, and he was happy to ship several tons of stuff the NHS didn't need to his new prospective trading partner, Evil Emperor Xi. The Chinese were having a bit of bother running out of their own made-in-China protective piffle. This was due to the made-in-China, Chinese Sniffle causing havoc in Chinese hospitals in China. It was the least the UK could do, Boris felt. Xi had promised to get cracking on the biggest trade deal the world had ever seen, and if you couldn't trust an evil emperor, then who could you trust?

Life at Chevening was by no means hermetically sealed. The ancient windows rattled like Churchill's knee joints due to shortcomings in slack seventeenth-century double glazing regulations, and it meant that the minor irritations of life had every chance of intruding.

He'd opened his red box to find several guttering flyers from Mr Bennett and his sons, along with a carefully worded yet heavily redacted 125-word version of an article in the *Telegraph*. The press Johnnies were asking tricky questions about Musty. Who had paid for the rental of villa Whiff-Whaff, and what did David Ross, the phone bloke, have to do with it, and why hadn't he declared it as a gift, and was the villa only available because a family from Dunstable had been forcibly evicted? This was the problem with 'ands'. They tended to pool their resources and stack up in the most frightful places.

The two main reasons for Fucking Off to Chevening (FOC) were:

a) Sort out his divorce from assorted women. To his relief, Marty had informed him that this involved only one woman – The Wheeler Dealer.

b) Do something about the First Fiancée's pregnancy – people were beginning to notice.

Govicus the Traitor for instance, had passed Young Symonds on the stairs leading up to Stateroom #6 last week and couldn't pass by her. He had to reverse down and came bounding into the Downing Street office, secreting sweat and excitement. Somehow, Boris decided, Govicus must be fitted with a rip-cord or at least some kind of fail-safe device.

'Chiefy, I say Chiefy.'

'Yes, Michael?' Boris was always on guard whenever the traitor twisted his face into a vague approximation of a smile.

'It's Young Symonds, Chiefy.'

'What about her, Michael?'

'I couldn't get past her on the staircase and noticed the good lady was somewhat larger than she had been in our previous staircase encounters.'

'Meaning?'

'I think she may have been up to no good.'

'No good? What are you blathering on about, man?'

'Appalling un-ladylike activities, Chiefy.'

Boris had to do something. A man marooned in an ever-expanding universe of mistresses, wives, quickie-divorces, quickies in general, thigh squeezing and a myriad of gropings with the wives of world leaders could not easily explain it all away as a trifling mountain of piffle. Even with Govicus, he suspected, gullibility had its limits.

'She's preggers.'

'Preggers?'

'As in, with child. Having a baby.'

Govicus absorbed this horrifying information for a full five seconds before collapsing to the floor.

More 125-word summary print-outs hit the red box. Boris found the majority of them – which contained the buzz phrases and words such as VIRUS, software upgrade, COVID, strategic corporate branding, CORONAVIRUS, and linear power structure – completely and utterly, interminably dull. He waited until he'd polished off a hearty full English, then whizzed them through his 'delete anything I can't be arsed to read' steam-powered shredder, thoughtfully provided by Mr Rees-Mogg. For some inexplicable reason there were also some calling cards from the redoubtable Mr Bennett and his sons, politely enquiring after the parlous state of the Downing Street guttering.

The Cock called with news that there was a global shortage of PPE. They couldn't get hold of any more supplies, and the use-by dates on what they did have were ten years out of date.

'How can we fight a virus without any PPE, Matty?'

'I've thought of that, Chiefy. Why don't we print new labels with new dates and stick them on top of the old labels with old dates.'

It was a perfectly satisfactory outcome all round.

Boris was proud of The Cock. There was a man who could get things done yet was also dim-witted enough to believe anything he was told by Dom, or himself, and obediently feed it to the press and the house of commons.

As usual, the Marxist leader of Her Majesty's opposition was moaning about Boris not returning from his working holibobs to visit storm-hit areas and had the audacity to call him a part-time

Prime Minister. That was a bit rich coming from a bloke whose idea of PMQ's was reading out letters from members of the working classes. Corbyn was so inexorably useless that he qualified for a position in the cabinet. Thinking about it, Boris wondered why Dom hadn't thought of that. Besides, he was already in a storm-hit area. Dilyn had pissed in Young Symonds' welly bobs, so there was zero chance of going out in this weather, even if he wanted to…which he didn't, thanks for asking.

The most annoying issue he had to deal with was the relentless guff that bubbled to the surface about him and an American business lady, Jennifer Arcurri. He only had a single A4 sheet with 125 words to go on in his red box, but it didn't look good. The whole furore dated back to his time as Lord Mayor of London. He'd told Young Symonds that the silver dancing pole in his study was a rare eighteenth-century family heirloom, a genuine Arcurri, believed to be Italian in origin and quite possibly made in Verona.

Under close questioning while out on a rowing boat on the Chevening lake, Young Symonds held up a copy of *The Mail* and pointed at the front page. The evidence against was nothing if not incriminating.

'WTAF, Boris. Tell me the truth, you serial shagging bastard.'

Anyone who has tried this fessing-up stuff will tell you it's almost impossible while a frenzied woman is holding your head underwater, and the ship is in imminent danger of capsizing.

Young Symonds was not in the mood for excuses. All she wanted were the stone-cold facts. She slammed his head back into the water. His arms flailed. The only result of her overly dramatic interrogation method was a long line of bubbles bobbing along the lake's surface. Despite three dunkings, the taste of the water wasn't improving. She yanked on the mop of wet hair, bringing Boris back above a furious churn of water.

'That fucking dancing pole is hers, isn't it, you philandering scumbag,' she said with self-satisfied vigour.

Chevening was supposed to be a retreat from the outside world and the tornados now sweeping across the country, but it was no retreat from the bruising fists of the maniacal Young Symonds. He had already resigned himself to a tragic yet heroic death. Perhaps he was the reincarnation of Lord Byron. He coughed up a mouthful of brackish lake water. It was like plummeting to earth in an Elon Musk spaceship only to be told that the batteries had run out, some trainee had forgotten to pack the parachutes because they were updating their 'Twitter' profile, and the AI-designed heatshield claimed diminished responsibility. There were undoubted side effects from the result of having your head forcibly arranged in a face-down, underwater position.

'It was years ago,' squawked Boris, spitting out half the lake. He was attempting to use the time-honoured *Back to The Future* gambit. This worked on the basis that life was very different a long time ago, and he could shag anyone he wanted if he had it in writing that it wasn't a close relative.

'Tell me everything about that blond-haired American bimbo with a face full of teeth. And trust me, I mean everything.'

Boris spilt the proverbial beans. The meetings, the dalliances, the Hi Ho Silver Lining Pole Dancing song, introducing her to people in the right places, helping develop her 'business' and so on and yada and double yada. She stood him up and thanked him for his honesty. She patted his cheeks affectionately and put her arms around his neck.

Just as he thought that all's well that ends well and everything was forgiven, she kneed him hard and unapologetically in the gentleman's testicular area. He collapsed in a heap of pain and brain-paralysing anguish, but then again, what was new?

Churchill War Rooms

In a dramatic break with blue-sky, feng shui, watsu massage, levelled-up thinking, Boris had arranged for a cabinet meeting with the new cabinet to be held underground in Churchill's war rooms.

The most notable change was a distinct lack of Spreadsheet Saj – a man last seen leaving Downing Street with two darts protruding from his forehead. In his place was a replacement sums expert – Spreadsheet Rishi. He'd been manoeuvred into place by the grandees. Spreadsheet Saj had made a joke in the house about Cummings and goings and, for his pains, had been banished from the kingdom, his lands confiscated, and his children sold to the church.

As custom decreed, Boris arrived after everyone else to a fanfare of Flugelhorns. The room was so crowded he had to be carried over the heads of his ministers and crowd surfed to his place in the middle of the immense, green baize oval table.

'Morning, everyone; I'd like to extend a jolly warm welcome to Spreadsheet Rishi, who has taken over from Spreadsheet Saj.

Spreadsheet Rishi is stonkingly wizzy-wizzo at sums and has full use of the nation's debit card.'

This was met with an enthusiastic burst of applause.

'We need to catch up with a few bits and bobs that passed me by on my working holiday at Chevers. Michael, if you'd kindly do the honours,' said Boris, gesturing to Govicus the traitor.

Govicus had formed a theory that the faster he talked, the more important he sounded. He'd developed this technique and deployed it during his morning jogs when he arrived back at his house to find a mob of reporters camped outside.

'First thing on today's agenda, Chiefy, is Storm Tosser, which has caused some damage in some parts of our great nation.'

'I'm led to believe it was a foreign storm,' remarked Priti Patel ominously.

'Was there any damage in Toffshire?' asked Boris.

Govicus flicked through his notes.

'Some unfortunate consequences, Chiefy. Lady Von Richtho-fens's green wheelie bin was blown over,' he replied. 'Emergency services were soon on the scene.'

The defence bloke lifted his head from a large book balanced on his knee.

'I've put the army on standby,' he said and immediately went back to the book.

'That's good news. I'll pay her a visit,' said Boris.

The cabinet reacted in horror.

'That really wouldn't do,' said Govicus.

'Bad form, I'm afraid, Chiefy,' put in The Cock.'

'110% Rah Rah with that,' agreed Patel.

'It's not the done thing for a Tory prime minister to be seen visiting anyone either during a crisis or in the immediate aftermath. It would send out all the wrong signals,' cooed Raab softly.

The room fell silent, the cabinet giving Boris due time to allow the ramifications to sink home. Into the eerie vacuum of thought stepped The Truss who decided the moment was right to unveil a brand-new Brexit trade deal pamphlet. She shared it with the table.

'I took the opportunity to close a trade deal with the Welsh, Chiefy, for British Wellington Boots, British umbrellas, British Cornish pasties, British Yorkshire puddings, British potted plants, and not forgetting British fridge magnets.'

Boris stared at the pamphlet. Foolhardy notions about visiting Lady Von Richthofen evaporated. He pumped his fists.

'Stonkingly superb stuff. We can safely blame those socialists masquerading as an opposition party for the arrival of Storm Tosser and the upending of her ladyship's bin. Matty, how are things progressing on the Chinese Sniffle front?'

'The Sniffle is creating havoc in China and Italy, Chiefy. Our intrepid leaflet defence forces (LDF) seem to be holding the fort at Heathrow. The virus only seems to be infecting foreigners, which is excellent news all around.'

Cummings eyed The Cock. It was one thing talking about swaying hearts and minds but generally the swayees needed to have a mind in the first place.

'I went to a top-secret SAGE meeting, Chief,' he said.

Boris looked surprised. 'Cripes, Dommers. I thought you said they were so jolly hush-hush the people in it don't even know they are in it.'

'That's correct, Chief, but I had a tip-off.'

'Excellent, Dom. So, what do they know?'

'I'm sworn to secrecy. It's all jolly hush-hush, Chief.'

'I know that, but we need to know what they know,' said Boris, somewhat unsatisfied with this reply from his chief senior special adviser. 'The Chief Exec of the NHS claimed there were no cases anywhere whatsoever in the UK and we have a stonkingly superb system for testing and tracing contacts.'

'If you ask me,' said The Cock, 'the no cases scenario doesn't sound massively likely.'

"Exactly, Matty, that's why I've moved our cabinet meetings to the war rooms. I don't trust the boffins. We need to be prepared.'

Cummings scratched his head. Somehow his delicately worked machinations had manoeuvred him towards the wrong end of the wrong end of the wrong stick. Something was wrong. Very wrong indeed. He needed to get away and analyse the data flows as a matter of urgency. He was borderline flustered.

'But Professor Whitty shared his figures with me.'

'Perhaps he made them up,' said Boris.

Govicus finished his cup of Fortnum & Mason's bespoke blend Earl Grey tea and delicately dabbed his lips with the header page of a government white paper.

'Is that it? SAGE's world-beating qualities of rigorous scientific examination are supposed to make us the envy of the world, and now they appear to be making things up as they go along. How did Professor Whitty explain that one away?'

'He admitted that he might be getting it confused with SAGE's research into the temperature of Whitehall coffee. However, he assured the committee that his blueberry muffin was pillow-soft, light and airy, and he'd beaten his personal best on the Rubik's Cube.'

This caught the attention of the defence bloke. He lifted his head from page 519 of *Jane's Fighting Ships*.[13]

'What's the dear boy's time?' he enquired.

'Three minutes, twenty-six seconds, precisely.'

This was greeted by approving nods and spasmodic murmurs from around the table.

'So, has our world-beating Sniffle testing system been successful?' asked Boris.

The Cock pumped his fists. 'Stonkingly successful, Chiefy. It found half a dozen cases, plus Priti's mobile phone as a bonus.'

'Rah Rah,' shouted Priti. 'I lost the bally thing while serving some drowning migrants with deportation papers,' she said with a disconcerting level of relish.

'Incredible. Some practical application at last,' said Raab.

Spreadsheet Rishi's fingers were little more than a blur across the keyboard of his Japanese desktop scientific calculator. 'I've crunched the numbers. Our world-beating Coronavirus testing system has cost us £26 million of Her Madge's pounds to find Priti's phone. That breaks down at almost twenty-six million pounds for each phone it finds.'

---

13 Entity recognition, capability, and threat assessments.

Raab thumped the table with his fists. 'Worth every penny, I'd say. Unbeatable value for the British taxpayer.'

'More good news, Chiefy. Our sciencey boff chums at Nervtag have kept the moderately moderate threat level to moderate,' said The Cock.

The Defence Bloke coughed and glared at The Cock.

'There is no moderately moderate level is there? It stands to reason that it must be simply "moderate". You can't have moderately moderate.'

'I can only be guided by the science,' retorted The Cock.

That was a good one, thought Cummings. He made a mental note.

Boris felt angry and frustrated. 'That's this Nervtag's job, is it? Announce the national threat level wily-nily and get everyone's wires crossed?'

'They're only an advisery thingy, I think, Prime Minister, nothing to worry about,' said Cummings, unaware that a string of dribble was hanging from his jaw.

Boris was full-on red in the face. 'We can't have a bunch of scientific boffo's making things up on the hoof. I'm raising the UK threat level from moderate to moderately high, back down to moderately low and then boosted to moderate.'

'That will give them some richly deserved mud in the eye,' said Raab.

'Consider it done, Chiefy. I'll notify the appropriate authorities at the *Cleethorpes Gazette* to publish the notification in the small ads as usual,' said 'The Cock'.

'Good stuff, Matty,' said Cummings, who placed both hands behind his head and his bare feet on the table. 'Anything else to report?'

'It's officially our position not to give a proverbial monkeys about the difficulties the Chinese and Italians have managed to create for themselves.'

Boris ruffled his hair from back to front – a sure sign it was time to wrap things up.

'Thanks very much, everyone. As you all know, I've been working flat out and around the clock since returning from Chevers, so I'll be taking the weekend off at Chequers.'

Raab was taken aback. His shark eyes rolled back in their sockets, and specks of blood appeared on his fangs. This was, after all, a man permanently in charge of a teeth-grinding inner rage.

'Chequers?'

'Yes, Chequers. Ye Gods, man. Am I conversing in Latin?'

'I'm sorry, Chiefy, but I believe that Lady Raab and I secured the weekend via Booking.com. A large double, with a four-poster bed and flat-screen TV. Breakfast included and free parking.'

Boris eased back in his chair.

'I'm sorry to pull rank, Raaby, but as PM, I can, and indeed have, overridden all previous bookings.'

'The official caravan at Camber Sands is free,' said Cummings helpfully. 'All you have to do is fill out a CS1 requisition form.'

Raab nodded quietly. The Camber Sands option would not alleviate his somewhat dark mood. However, he was nothing if not obedient and instinctively knew when it was time to sit quietly and wag his tail.

'On a final note, folks,' said Boris, 'I've decided to take the Sniffle a taddly bit more seriously, jump into the pool, and take full control. I will chair a COBRA first thing on Monday morning.'

This caught the cabinet unawares. There were gasps of shock. Even Cummings had to grip the arms of his chair. Someone must have spiked the Earl Grey, Raab decided. After all, the chief had not bothered turning up for the first five COBRAS of the Sniffle thingy.

'By "first thing," I do, of course, mean eleven o'clock,' said Boris.

The room breathed a collective sigh of relief.

March 2020

3 March
Upper Library, 10 Downing Street

Boris took his morning coffee and two plates of organic free-range croissants in the library. He gazed up at the bookcase crammed with leather-bound novels, imbuing it with a colonial charm. It was always tempting to squirt them with a water pistol as he'd done with young Smythe-Farquhar-Smythe back in his Eton days. It was a handsome collection of the finest classical literature known to civilisation. Shortly after moving into Downing Street, he had a word about the bookcase filing system in Marty's shell-like. Marty clicked his fingers, assorted underlings were pressed into service and works by Homer, Virgil, Cicero, Aristotle, Dan Brown, and Ovid now rubbed shoulders somewhat incongruously with classic contemporary writing such as:

Seventy-Two Virgins – Boris Johnson
The Dream of Rome – Boris Johnson
The Churchill Factor – Boris Johnson
Top Totty in Jolly Fast Cars – Boris Johnson

TTJFC was the one where he compared a young lady driving a Ferrari to riding a racehorse. He was surprised it hadn't been banned. That would have blown sales through the roof, particularly in the lucrative overseas markets.

Marty popped his head around the door. Cummings followed with a camera slung around his neck and carrying a tripod over his shoulder to film Boris's morale boosting video address to the nation.

'Congrats on Saturday's happy announcement, sir.'

'Thank you, Marty. The First Fiancée and I decided to keep it jolly hush-hush until now. Dom suggested it would be as good a time as any to announce an engagement and a baby in one fell swoop.'

'It certainly helped keep the bloody Sniffle off the front pages,' Cummings pointed out.

'I couldn't agree more, sir,' agreed Marty, as ever mystified by the big white one's needy dependence on his chief senior special adviser.

'I pootled into a boffin factory yesterday on my way back from Chequers.'

'Really, sir. What did you find?' inquired Marty.

'One of the boffo wallahs told me you can't actually see the Sniffle.'

'It can't be that dangerous then, can it, sir,' answered Marty with impeccable Whitehall logic. 'We all thought it would be the size of a tennis ball.'

'Exactly,' sniffed Boris. Hardly the doom-laden pestilence they keep rabbiting on about.'

Cummings decided it was wise to steer clear of this conversation. He fiddled about with the camera and attached it to the tripod. Armed with his trusty laser protractor, he took precise measurements. These were based on the hourly feng shui, blue-sky satellite data emailed direct to the Dombox by NASA.

Three minutes later, Boris launched into his video message and the greatest speech in his career.

He told everyone that he'd just chaired a meeting of COBRA, and there was a stonkingly superb new strategy for dealing with the Sniffle. Furthermore, an action plan would be put in place when the time was right to put it in place, and it suited him to put it in place. The government was following the science; the Sniffle was jolly mild, and there was no need to panic as long as everyone washed their hands and sang Happy Birthday at the same time. He finished it off with the immortal lines:

'We shall fight it in the wine bars of Islington, we shall fight it on the zip-wires and in the fridges, we shall fight it on the playing fields of Eton, we shall fight it around the dancing poles and in the Harrods food hall.'

After finishing his address, which made him feel jolly important and chock full of baked beans, there was an almighty commotion outside. Boris, Dom, and Marty rushed to the window. A scene of pandemonium greeted them. The street was under assault from a blizzard of flashing blue lights, wailing sirens, and high-pitched screaming.

Boris bounded down the staircase and out into the Downing Street mayhem. It was clear that something catastrophic had happened. He saw flagship BBC political reporter Laura Knuessberg being hurried towards an ambulance on a stretcher. A paramedic was attempting to pry a microphone out of her hands, but in the spirit of diehard BBC journalism, she held on for grim death. Boris hurried over.

'Goodness Laura, what on earth happened?' he asked.

'Don't Laura me, you utter bastard,' gasped Laura. She sounded as if she were breathing her last. Boris loathed the communists who ran the BBC, but he did have a soft spot for Laura. She was an unstoppable force in the world of clear-sighted, asking awkward questions journalism, despite her being Scottish.

'I'm sorry, dear girl, but I'm at a complete loss,' he said.

'You should ask yourself, Prime Minister.'

'You're blaming me? This is my fault?'

'Another irresponsible Johnson action, as if Brexit wasn't enough of a reckless, barrel-scraping exercise.'

'Sorry, old girl, I don't know what you're going on about. Are you on medication?'

'It's nothing to do with my anti-Bullshit pills. When will you claim responsibility for this attack on a free press, Prime Minister?'

'I've done nothing wrong, Laura.'

'Minutes ago, you were broadcasting to the nation.'

'Indeed, and looking totally buff if I may say so myself.'

'What did you start off by saying?'

'I merely stated that I'd just chaired a COBRA and showed everyone my attendance certificate, lanyard and badge.' He dangled the lanyard in Laura's face. Her eyes went wide. They sank back into their sockets and flicked wildly from side to side. Her body convulsed and twitched.

'You chaired a COBRA meeting? You never chair COBRA meetings. Have you any idea of the carnage and devastation you've caused?' she cried.

'I had to take control, my dear girl. The boffins change their minds every few minutes and Hancock has somehow ordered forty pallets of Cyan printer ink from Turkey.'

Boris placed his arms behind his back and beat a slow retreat to the front door. Being blamed for something that was 100% not your fault was another good reason to add to the steadily increasing list of good reasons not to be PM.

The Same Time as the Previous Time
Downing Street Rose Garden

Young Symonds stood in the middle of the Rose Garden, trying to block out the appalling hullabaloo going on outside Number 10. There was something far more pressing on her mind. She raised an early eighteenth-century flintlock musket to her shoulder and took careful aim.

'I hope you appreciate that this is nothing personal. The court's verdict was unanimous. Guilty on all charges, including that of high treason and sedition. The sentence was found to be legal and fully in accordance with Her Madge's British law.'

Thirty feet across the garden, tied to Mr Rees-Mogg's steam-powered wheelbarrow and trussed up like famed Hollywood serial killer, Dr Hannibal Lector, was Larry the Cat. Beamish's investigation had left no stone unturned. Cat hair was found on the sofa, and following stringent DNA analysis, it was matched to one

Larry the Cat, Resident Mouser of Number 10 Downing Street. The death sentence seemed a bit harsh, but then the crime was so severe that it fully warranted the ultimate punishment. Larry would pay a terrible price for his heinous crimes, misdemeanours, and unwarranted attack on the £73,359 Yamamoto Zebra print eco-sofa. Young Symonds didn't give half a shit about the cat's constitutional rights.

The musket was ancient, a relic from HMS *Victory*, but it was the nearest thing Young Symonds could find to a weapon in the building. She squinted down the barrel.

'Any last words, you sick excuse for a bloody cat?' Young Symonds demanded. She cupped her ear. 'No? Well, I thought not.'

Larry listened to all this in startled silence.

Young Symonds' fingers curled around the trigger. The hammer dropped back. Larry stared back at her with uncomprehending eyes. Was this fucking it? He'd been a faithful cat all his life. The only time he ever put a paw wrong was when he mistook Mrs May's William Morris floral print flats for an unwanted intruder and took a massive shit in them. She wasn't best pleased when she slipped them on for a meeting with the orange Sultan of Vegas, Donald Trump, and caused a major security alert. At first, it was difficult for Mrs May to work out where the smell was coming from – her shoes or his sunburnt eminence.

Admittedly, Larry spent a lot of time thinking up convoluted plots to murder his current master in the goriest way imaginable. However, it was one thing to daydream about committing a ghastly deed and quite another to pull it off. He knew who the real cat hair/coffee/chocolate truffle villain was, but now he'd have to take that secret to the grave.

What happened next was so fast that Young Symonds could barely grasp what was happening. Beamish rushed across the garden, scooped up Larry and dived to the ground as the musket fired and a lead ball whistled clean through his standard 'made in China' bulletproof Whitehall issue briefcase.

'Beamy, what in God's name are you doing?' yelled Young Symonds, a veritable cauldron of rampant emotion.

'Saving this cat from a grave injustice, ma'am,' said Beamish, picking himself and Larry off the grass.

'You've interfered in the execution of a lawfully executed execution. This is nothing short of high treason.' Young Symonds' voice sounded harsh, strident, and borderline shrieky. A bit like Mrs Thatcher if she were trying to escape from a tumble dryer 'accidentally' switched to its maximum turbo 4500 rpm setting.

'Larry did nothing wrong, ma'am,' Beamish said quietly, softly stroking Larry, who was now quite prepared to sue someone over his PTSD.

Young Symonds lowered the smoking musket.

'Then who was it? Who defiled my gorgeous eco-designer sofa?' she demanded.

Beamish examined the hole in his briefcase. Outsourcing to China still had quality control issues. He snapped the locks and took out a miniature spy camera.

'It looks like any normal Soviet spy camera, ma'am, but it's a British spy camera. The crafty Soviets disguised it as a Soviet spy camera, then re-disguised it again as a British spy camera. We then disguised it again to look like a Soviet spy camera, to make the Soviets think it was a British spy camera—'

'Yes, yes, yes, Beamy, it all sounds awfully complicated and resoundingly dastardly,' said Young Symonds vaguely.

'Indeed, ma'am, but it did an excellent job filming the events that unfolded on the pink zebra print sofa on the morning in question. Mr Cummings removed the CCTV cameras but failed to anticipate that his every move would be recorded by a Soviet spy camera masquerading as a British spy camera masquerading as a Soviet spy camera.'

He showed Young Symonds the footage: The spectre like grandees departing, Boris upending his coffee, the tsunami of blind panic, Cummings tearing out of the room, returning with Larry and rubbing him vigorously into the plush eco-fabric sofa.

'It's utterly revolting, Beamy. Boris spilt his coffee, which could happen to anyone, especially Boris, but Cummings used poor Larry to sponge everything up.'

'And this is from the footage taken from the CCTV footage covering the rear door and external areas.'

'He put him in a sack? My God, is that a van Cummings threw him into?'

'Larry was rescued from the back of Ms Patel's slammed immigration van.'

'Slammed?'

'Heavily modified. For drifting purposes, ma'am.'

'Well, I daresay she needs that on the high seas.'

Young Symonds wiped a tear from her eye and helped Beamish cut Larry free.

'I'm so sorry, Larry. Now I know it wasn't you. How will you ever forgive me? I suggest treaties every night in the Downing Street flat, and I promise we will work together to bring down the evil Machiavellian mastermind.

Larry liked the sound of this. He purred softly and rubbed himself against her legs.

House of Commons

Boris was positively bouncing with slightly feigned enthusiasm as he always was these days. Whenever he and his crack team were getting ready to bedazzle Her Madge's useless opposition in the house the adrenalin flowed like the confluence of the Ganges. He watched Raab and The Cock go through their elaborate fitness routines replete with squats, lunges, and thrusts.

The week had gone jolly well for Boris. He'd finally got the hang of this COBRA meeting malarkey, and it was a stonkingly superb way of demonstrating his powers of leadership and that he was in control without overdoing it.

Naturally, chairing a Cobra or two was a massive inconvenience, but he found them a bit of a diddle-doddle and certainly no worse than preparing his case to the Eton Debating Society. If your foe was Smythe-Fotherington-Smythe, you needed to put your prep on a war footing.

He invited everyone to speak, told them he'd act on their recommendations and put the Kick it into the Long Grass strategy in place. This came under the jolly hush-hush Do Fuck All policy umbrella, but was slightly more PR friendly, albeit for reasons that weren't always immediately obvious.

The Cock had his face buried in a glossy software sales brochure. It took him a moment and a well-aimed elbow from Raab to finish what he was reading and realise that the chief was talking to him.

He stuttered into life with: 'Absolutely, Chiefy, people should go about their business as bloody usual.' He was pleased he'd thrown the 'bloody' into the mix. Not for nothing was he gaining a reputation for being a cabinet badass.

'Some of our sciencey boffin Johnnies feel that we shouldn't be letting big sporting events go ahead. The opposition will be raising the point today,' said Raab.

'Stuff and blubbering nonsense,' said Boris, angry at the notion that something so important and vital could possibly be stopped. 'I've got ringside tickets to see England give some far inferior nation a damn good thrashing at the rugger,' he added. 'If the Sniffle expects a full-scale, Dunkirk style retreat, we're not going to give it the satisfaction.'

'Shaking hands as well,' said Cummings.

'The SAGE lunatics are talking about stopping people shaking hands, as well as banning large gatherings,' said Boris. 'They say the French have stopped large gatherings, and we should do the same. I knocked that into a cocked hat by telling Whitty to put down his Rubik's Cube.'

'Bloody Whitty and his boffins say there is no evidence that gatherings make any difference to anything whatsoever.'

Boris was outraged. 'It's all part of the French underhand mind game strategy. They are well aware that only foreigners are badly infected with Le Sniffle and want low attendance because they know they stand no chance against eighty thousand Englishmen singing Swing Low, Sweet Chariot.'

'SAGE wants us to shut our borders as well. They're out of control, Chiefy,' said The Cock, in between sneaky peeks at his brochure. 'They've spent ten minutes making some models of computers and are now saying everyone will die unless we do something,'

'Typical French,' said Govicus the Traitor, 'never a good word to say about anyone.'

'I've been mulling things over,' said Boris. 'If this bloody thing spreads any more, and there is, as they say, a sustained transmission of infections, even in this great country of ours, I recommend that we develop a strategy of protecting the vulnerable and all jolly bloody jaldi jaldi.'

Normally, with Boris, unless you paid incredibly close attention and were good at taking notes, there was a good chance that most of what he said would pass you completely by. However, this was one of those rare occurrences when what came out of his mouth was crystal clear and made sense. The Cock and Cummings sat up and took notice. Jolly bloody jaldi jaldi meant things needed to happen even faster than jolly bloody pronto tonto. Something had lit up in the Chief's brain that would require their full attention – the first time, in fact, since Brexit Day.

The Cock found it deeply puzzling that, at times, it felt as though the Big White Chief didn't want to be a Chief at all. He took a deep breath and plunged right in.

'The vulnerable, Chiefy? Do you mean the riff-raff, the hoi-polloi, and anyone not living in Toffshire?' he asked reverentially.

'Lordy, no, I mean us,' said Boris. 'The ruling class, the hereditary elite.'

Cummings and The Cock exchanged looks varying in degrees from moderate WTF to moderately high WTAF.

'Us, Chief?' hazarded Cummings.

Boris pootled a hand through his rebellious mop of floppy upper-crust hair.

'Yes, ordinary people who have been to Eton and Oxford, politicians, special advisers and above all else, prime ministers. Vulnerable people like us should be an absolute priority and protected from any unspeakable diseases that ignore leaflets and rudely sneak into our green and pleasant land without obtaining written permission,' said Boris, warming to his theme. 'If we cark it, who is going to save the country?'

'Will this protect the vulnerable scheme extend to ex-wife's, partners, and tiresome progeny, Chief?'

'I don't see why not. We can vote if you feel strongly about it, Dommers.'

'The boffins are muttering about more stringent measures,' said The Cock. Lockdown seems to be their word of the moment. Something other countries are doing.'

'I've said I'll take action when I see fit. I'm not taking action because the rabble across the channel deems it necessary to take action. This is not North Korea or Liverpool bloody council. We do not do 'ockdown, we stand and fight, or close the wall up with our English dead.'

'No, Chiefy, absolutely not,' grovelled Hancock.

'Can't ask for much more than that, Chief,' agreed Cummings. 'In the meantime, the slogan should be BUSINESS AS BLOODY USUAL in capital letters,' he suggested.

'Business as blusteringly rah-rah businessy normal,' said Priti Patel.

'Very well, so we have some big sporting events coming up. Are we au fait with letting them go ahead?' asked Boris.

'Can't see it doing any harm, Chiefy. Rugger, Footie, Cheltenham, and massive pop concerts should all go ahead.'

The Cock flicked through his bundle of briefing papers and eyed Cummings carefully. Fortunately, the great Svengali was nodding his enormous egg-shaped head.

'We can tell them to strap bottles of hand sanitiser to the backs of the bobbos,' he suggested helpfully.

'At the pop concert?'

'No, At Cheltenham.'

'Cheltenham has to go ahead at all costs,' said Boris. 'Young Symonds has fifty pounds on *Donkeys Dangle*r at twenty-five to one in the three fifteen.'

Several ministers hastily made a note.

Patel sighed. 'Are we letting foreign Madrid fans from Spain come to Liverpool? La Liga has stopped their games of association football on account of mass outbreaks of the Sniffle.'

Boris thumped the table. 'I'm not letting a minor Sniffle stop people enjoying their freedom. That's typical of the weak-kneed, Spanish bed-wetters. Trust me, I know what to do with those Tapas sniffing Johnnies, and that's to send their Armada chappies to the bottom of my bath three times a week.'

Cummings raised his left eyebrow and positioned it in the customary 'quizzical' position. 'So, Chief, if posh people and politicians are now included in our vulnerable category, what happens to all the poor people?'

'Between occasional breaks in his record attempt on the Rubik's Cube world record, Professor Whitty said it's OK to let the Sniffle run riot. He called it herd immunity,' said The Cock.

'Herd immunity it jolly well is,' roared Boris. 'Real Madrid? Bring them on.'

'So, we're not wavering from our overall jolly hush-hush DO FUCK ALL strategy, are we, Chief?'

'Absolutely not, Dommers. 'Do Fuck All' is our raison d'etre, and there's nothing whatsoever to worry about. We'll bat this virus away in no time.' Boris waved his fists. It was time for a suitable rabble-rousing speech: 'Each Trojan that is master of his heart, let him to field.'

Cummings, Raaby, The Cock, Govicus the traitor, and Patel pumped their fists, and followed their fearless commander-in-chief on his epic charge into the House of Commons.

A Week or Two Later
Downing Street Flat

Boris was terminally bored with endless blah blah meetings featuring an endless stream of endlessly blah blah people. Quickly spotting the early warning tell-tale signs of her IWH becoming Boris Grump, the CEO of Tetchy Inc., Young Symonds, did her best to cheer him up and encouraged him to stick to their grand plan.

'We must do it, Bumble. Staying on our hymn sheet is the only way our exit strategy will pay off.'

'How can I be expected to work on my novels, sink armadas, or finish constructing my model of a 1956 Routemaster when I'm disrupted every five seconds with outrageous demands on my time? No wonder Caesar sodded off to build a bridge across the Rhine after telling everyone he was popping outside for a quick fag.'

'What ails thee, my lord?' she asked calmly, noting that the thin-skinned-ometer was deep in the red.

'Here, this turned up out of the blue.'

He handed her a note. Young Symonds read it out aloud.

'Crisis meeting. Strangers Bar. This morning, 11.30 a.m. signed, the Boffs.'

'Another bloody meeting. This prime minister stuff is getting out of hand. The abominable scientists will be ruling the roost, I expect.'

'Don't implement anything you don't want to implement, darling.'

'Exactly, Sweetpea. I'm not a stage magician.'

Several Moans and Gripes Later
Strangers Bar, House of Commons

Boris found himself at the bar with a pint of Old Thatch in his hand. He had to admit that he missed having a semi-naked Ms McVey on tap, whiff-whaffing him with a palm frond. Perhaps that was why he felt so irritable, a feeling exacerbated by a severe Downing Street drought of boundless bonhomie and a severe shortage of motivational sales patter. The Cock attempted to speak, but he had temporarily managed to get one of his thumbs stuck in his eye.

'We need to talk about herd immunity, Prime Minister,' said Professor Whitty. Beside him, Professor Vallance nodded his agreement. Boris decided to attack and put the scientists to the sword. He pointed his pint at Professor Whitty.

'This herd immunity business of yours hasn't worked at all, and according to a man I spoke to on the telly, it could mean that everyone dies.'

'Of course, I will deny I agreed with it in the first place, my liege.'

'The old plausible deniability routine,' said Cummings. "I'm not sure anyone will buy that, Prof.'

Whitty kept schtum. His eyes focused on his Rubik's Cube.

'Herd immunity. I can't imagine a more ridiculous idea if I tried,' said The Cock.

Professor Whitty stared desperately around the bar, hoping for support and someone to back him up. None was forthcoming. The cabinet was a malignant ecosystem. It clung together despite loathing the very sight of itself. By this time, The Cock had managed to extricate his thumb.

'You've stood between a pair of stout union jacks, Chiefy, and told the great British public that it's nothing to worry about, and you were listening to the science, even though these boffo blighters won't say a dickie. So why bother with them now?'

'Good point, Matty.' Cummings was on his feet, a glass of prossey in his hand. He gestured in the direction of the reticent scientists. 'These moaning nimbies don't even like you shaking hands, Prime Minister. A prime minister should be free to wipe his hands on his underpants, then shake hands should he feel the urge.'

The rest of the ministers erupted in applause.

While they clapped, Boris's mind went into overdrive. All the salient facts churned around the outer perimeter of his brain. He was seized by one of Dom's blue-sky, feng shui, watsu eureka moments and banged his table hard with both fists.

'The only way to fight the Sniffle is to stick to our DO FUCK ALL, do nothing policy. We're not going to let a Chinese Sniffle restrict our freedoms. We will give battle.'

Whitty's ears pricked up. This was not good at all. This was worse than not good at all, although he couldn't think what was possibly worse than not good at all. Moderately not good? All he could muster was a half-hearted, 'But people will think we're doing nothing.'

Cummings rubbed his hands together.

'Exactly. We must continue with the scientifically proven Do Fuck All strategy and let the Sniffle run riot. The longer we can drag it out, the more we generate a state of blind panic. At the right moment, when we finally do something, people will worship us like Gods.'

'Absolutely stonkingly brilliant, Dommers,' said Boris.

Professor Whitty didn't share Boris's enthusiasm but felt he'd better say something. After all, he didn't want his scientific budget reduced any further. He had his eye on a new microscope; a state-of-the-art 5000 x magnification, 3D organic Trinocular, with a 96-megapixel USB3.0 Camera, LCD screen, Bluetooth, and the capability of playing the opening title theme from *Game of Thrones*.

'We can say that closing schools, banning big gatherings, testing, and wearing facemasks is all a bit pointless,' he said.

'Like the bloody French and bloody Italians,' rah-rah'd Priti bloody Patel. She stood on her chair, clicked her heels, and unfurled a large Union Jack above her head. 'The snivelling cowards have already surrendered. They've called off the Italy against Ireland rugger game.'

Boris felt nauseous. 'Foreigners calling off rugger? They had no right to call off a game they hadn't even invented.'

'I've a good mind to take a swipe at the Italian cultural attaché with my number three hockey stick,' roared Patel.

The Cock squinted down at his notes. 'Didn't the WHO Johnnies say we *need* to do testing?'

'Needing isn't an absolute,' said Professor Whitty tetchily, trying to regain some scientific authority. This meeting was not going to plan. From going on the front foot, the scientific community was now flat on its back and about as off plan as you could get.

Cummings nodded. 'Everything has a loophole. However, I feel that just as an arse-covering exercise, we should have some plan for the record. You know, a join-the-dots statement along the lines of, 'We realise we need a lockdown and—'

Raab butted in. 'Let's not get hysterical, Dom. One minute you're happily kicking things into the long grass as part of our stonkingly brilliant Do Fuck All policy, and the next, you want to incarcerate us in some ghastly, and may I say, completely un-British, North Korean lockdown.'

Cummings was temporarily flustered by Raab's razor-sharp insight. An alarming popping noise was going off in the cata-combs behind his eyes. They glowed red, and he bravely fought off the urge to strangle the First Secretary of State with his own tie.

'I'm just throwing this out there. We should be prepared to move our world-beating prevaricate and delay measures a taddly bit forward.'

'What are we talking about, in terms of "taddly", Dommers?' asked Boris.

'The blue-sky reiki watsu crystals advise moderately taddly, Chief.'

Realising that 'moderately taddly' could cause instant cardiac arrest in the cabinet, Boris knew he had to dial down the tension somehow. He turned to Jacob Rees-Mogg.

'Moggy, a penny for your thoughts, my dear boy.'

Rees-Mogg puffed on his pipe, adjusted his monocle and tilted his top hat accoutrements slightly back on his head.

'One sincerely hopes that if we bring the delay measures a moderately taddly bit forward, and they manifest themselves as rules and restrictions, these will only apply to the lower orders.'

'We need restrictions,' said Professor Whitty, stroking the underside of his chin, which was still ringed with a burn mark from when he rested it on a Bunsen burner earlier that morning.

'Restrictions?' barked Raab.

'Out of the question,' spluttered Priti Patel. 'It's communism through the back door.'

They were all on their feet, pushing and shoving the professors, who fought back gamely. Boris sat back and enjoyed the sport. The shit was stirred. The tectonic plates of the grand plan were grinding splendidly into place. It wouldn't be long before the grandees turned up at his front door with their begging bowls, pleading with him to retire as a brave hero, the finest leader the nation has ever had. He watched his minister's brawl with the boffins and then with each other with a benign yet detached curiosity.

The month rolled on, and the virus quicksand slowly bogged down the wheels of Boris's strategy. The top man at the WHO, Thuycdides Bejaysus, officially declared the Sniffle as a global sniffledemic and the Italian mortality rate hit 10 per cent. The only good news was that Nadine Dorries became the first MP to contract the Sniffle.

Panic buying gripped the nation as the great unwashed thought it would be great to strip supermarkets of all essentials, especially toilet paper. Quite why a Mr and Mrs Shadbolt from Didsbury found it necessary to hoard 7260 rolls of Lidl Floralys standard white was anyone's guess.

After a week or more of the DO FUCK ALL policy, the prime minister was finally forced to announce a full lockdown. Due to the virus's icy grip he ordered people to work from home and to stay away from the office at all costs. Schools were shut as were all non-essential shops with the obvious exceptions of Harrods, Fortnum and Mason, and Selfridges. Britain plunged towards the dark spring of a dystopian nightmare. A virus invented in a Chinese lab had turned the country into a mirror image of the Chinese state.

The Cock claimed he was jolly sure that going into lockdown late hadn't led to a rise in people losing their lives, and he had a black eye from Professor Vallance to prove it. He protected the elderly by dragging them out of their hospital beds and sending them back to their flea-ridden care homes, without bothering to test whether the decrepit bed-hoggers had been infected with the Sniffle. This was The Cock's idea of a protective shield, a shield that first and foremost protected the health secretary. It all worked spiffingly well to save valuable bed space. It would also save on valuable NHS needles as they were more likely to break on the toughened, leathery skin of the old and economically useless.

When it was brought to their attention that NHS workers had to improvise and make PPE out of bin bags, the cabinet was delighted. It showed how resilient and fearless NHS lackeys were

and a stirring example of British pluck and gumption. The Cock
went on to instigate a weekly clap for the hardworking NHS.
Spreadsheet Rishi calculated that providing DIY protective clothing and handclaps instead of pay rises would save the exchequer
some £38bn. For his part, Boris was content with not doing very
much at all.

The only red buggeration flag on the horizon was the unlikely
event of someone important catching the Sniffle. Dom and his
underlings had successfully by-passed SAGE, what with all their
unreliable labs and 1970s computing equipment, and assured Boris that the chances of that happening were infinitesimal at best.
He still had the printout in his pocket, and the odds were there
in black and white – roughly one in 25 gazillion.

Bedroom, 11 Downing Street

The elegant strains of the Eton Boating Song reverberated
through Downing Street. It woke Young Symonds and Symonds
the Younger, who was currently renting her womb at a considerably lower than market rate. The baby saw it as an ideal opportunity to create pandemonium and, out of infantile duty, go on
the rampage and trampoline around the place as if possessed by a
hyperactive demon of the night. Young Symonds hated having
her sleep disturbed. She wasn't sure what was worse:

- The hideous boating song ringtone blasting through her
  IWH's phone
- Symonds the Younger's in-house gymnastics.
- Her IWH's breathless snorts.

She was pleased to announce that the winner was Number Three. She kicked her IWH mercilessly in the shins. He half-stirred and punched the air.

'Jennifer, dear girl. Once more around ye merry dancing pole, I prithee.'

Having her infinitely worse half wet dreaming about that American witch with more teeth than the entire population of Grimsby while being tortured by that dreadful Eton dirge emanating from his phone was enough to bring out the inner serial killer. With an almighty heave, she upended the slobbering mammoth out of the bed. He woke in a state of frothing indignation.

His eyes flashed. 'Good heavens above, Young Symonds, have you gone stark-staring mad?' He grabbed the bedstead and attempted to disentangle himself from the Yamamoto bed linen. 'This is like living with a manically depressed Bedouin.'

'You were dreaming about dancing around poles with that loopy American hag with the teeth. It's not good for the baby. Answer your bloody phone and change that hideous ringtone,' said Young Symonds belligerently.

Boris grabbed his phone.

'Dear God, it's the palace. On FACETIME!'

Her Madge's scowly face lit up his screen. Boris's union jack underpants took the opportunity to abandon their customary 'at ease' position and wound their way down towards his ankles.

'Fucking Lizziekins? On Facetime, at this time?' Young Symonds groaned and buried her face in a pillow.

Boris staggered out of the bedroom.

'Your most gracious majesty,' he croaked. 'To what do I owe—'

'One heard that, Boris, you miserable excuse for a gangrenous dung beetle. Tell that hysterical little floozy of yours that it's 'ma'am' or 'your most gracious majesty', not 'fucking Lizziekins'. Unless, of course, your precious Princess Nut Nut wishes to find herself bobbing up and down in Yokohama harbour. And pull your bloody underpants up, man.'

'Yes, ma'am, will do, ma'am. Begging your pardon, ma'am, but one sounds a taddly bit perturbed,' he said while gamely attempting to hoist his underpants back into a passable semblance of decency.

'More than a taddly bit, Johnson. Get yourself to the palace within the hour.'

'Forthwith, ma'am?'

'Forthwith, Young Master Boris.'

6.23 a.m.
Buckingham Palace Ballroom #3

After a death-defying drive in the bloody Fiat, with Schnipps at the helm, Boris found himself in the splendour of one of the palace's ballrooms – chandeliers, gold-leafed furniture and ornate mirrors the size of Bedfordshire. He was escorted to the end of a banqueting table by loyal and discerning royal equerry #11. Sixty feet away, Her Madge sat in throne #4 with a phone to her ear. Boris wasn't sure what to do until loyal and discerning royal equerry #7 handed him a ringing phone on a solid silver tray.

'It's her most gracious majesty,' said the equerry.

Boris looked at Her Madge. Her expression was firmly set to non-gracious, non-negotiable, full-on head removal mode. She waved her phone somewhat ungraciously, and Boris answered.

'About time too, Johnson. I'm not calling the Viceroy of India.'

'Yes, ma'am. Morning, ma'am.'

'It's Charles.'

'Let me guess, ma'am. Up to no good behind the organic free-range rhododendrons?'

'He's tested positive, you tiresome eejit.'

'A hearty congratulations, ma'am. I expect he needs a license to drive the royal combine harvester over the Duchy peasantry,' said Boris, half closing his eyes and wishing he was back in bed and dancing pole dreamland.

'Not for driving, for the bloody Sniffle. How dare you allow this Chinese foreigner into this glorious country of ours and contaminate the royal blood.'

'It's all utterly baffling, ma'am. We've handed out dozens of anti-Sniffle leaflets at the airports, and there's a phone number in case arrivals feel a taddly bit queasy. We're the best prepared nation on the planet, ma'am.'

'Be that as it may, your snivelling incompetence means I have two weeks of self-isolation to look forward to. What do you propose one and one's family do for coins of the realm?'

'Money, ma'am?'

'No social engagements mean no income from the souvenir trade and, thanks to you, the Windsor Castle Airbnb business can't accept paying guests.'

'Never fear, ma'am. I'm sure Spreadsheet Rishi will do some sums. You could apply for one of his whizzy business loans.'

'Business loans?' hissed Her Madge.

Her Madge's hiss was supernaturally terrifying, as many foreign dignitaries had found to their cost during her reign. Donald Trump wet himself after enduring a level five hiss when he dared to walk in front of Her Madge during an inspection of her favourite collection of shrunken heads. The hiss tied Boris's intestines in a tight knot and reduced him to a pile of quivering blonde blancmange.

'If anything happens to Charles, there will be consequences, Johnson. Grave consequences of the gravest nature. Consequences that could lead to a complete disintegration of monarchy, state, and empire.'

'I'm not sure I follow you, ma'am.'

'If Charles carks it, we all go down like ninepins.'

'I'm sure the country would be in safe hands, ma'am. In a worst-case scenario, Young Master Wills and Kate would do a stonkingly spiffy post-cark job.'

'Wills is far too wet to run a country. There are jellyfish with more backbone than him. Besides, how long do you think it would be before the dark forces made their move?'

'Their move, ma'am?' asked Boris, struggling to grasp the labyrinthine implications of all this tricky constitutional stuff.

'To take out Wills?'

It took Boris a few more seconds to absorb the horrors of the aforementioned labyrinthine implications.

'Surely not, ma'am?' spluttered Boris. 'They're brothers after all.'

'One assumes you've seen Beamish's dossier, DS/DC/696/b?'

'Of course, ma'am,' lied Boris through most of his teeth, 'but the evidence suggests…'

'Stuff the bloody evidence,' she raged. 'Where would this great nation be with Harry and his glue-sniffing concubine on the throne of England?'

'I'm sure Meghan would respect…'

'That scheming hussy-in-chief has no respect for anything, Young Master Boris. She has a direct line to Trump Towers. Before we know it, she'll turn the palace into a gruesome casino-hotel with neon signage and mega bonus slot machines in the khazi's. Do your bloody job, Johnson.'

With this, Her Madge smashed her phone on the gilded arm of Throne #5, the next throne along. The loyal and discerning royal equerries escorted Boris towards the exit. He was shell-shocked but relieved he'd resisted the inbuilt impulse to argue with Her Royal Madgeness. At times like this, it was like trying to deal with the ice queen of a Nordic saga who cast a dark and evil shadow over a fluffy kingdom of sunlit pastures.

A short time later
Bedroom, 11 Downing Street

Dazed by his early morning encounter, Boris returned to the bedroom. Young Symonds had propped herself up on a stack of Yamamoto pillows.

'The old dragon sounded perfectly vile.'

Boris grinned sheepishly. 'I think it demonstrates most adequately that the grand plan is coming together. When the grandees discover I've inadvertently allowed Charles to become infected, they will push me closer to the door.'

'Oh, Bumble,' said Young Symonds, punching him playfully on the arm, 'you're so frightfully clever sometimes, but I do so love you being PM. L.K Bennett give me a twenty per cent Downing Street discount on their new signature collection.'

Lockdown

With that playful punch on the shoulder, the country entered the twilight lockdown zone. The new normal was the new state-enforced abnormal. People couldn't see other people and were forced to follow a Kafkaesque series of 'on the hoof' rules and arcane restrictions. It was like living in a ditch, except most self-respecting ditches had a pub down one end. Anxiety levels rose from moderately low to record levels, and a pervading sense of all-round uselessness paralysed the government. It was a cloud of ineptitude, filled with a dense layer of nerve gas. Sniffle cases went through the roof and hospitals were swamped with sick patients. In time-honoured tradition the Do Fuck All policy meant that the government hadn't bothered to do much about the critical need for ventilators. Boris identified this as a problem and leapt into action In a rousing conference call with the great and good of British industry, he gave them a ventilator challenge and proudly announced Operation Last Gasp. The only bright spot on the horizon was that anyone already dead could rest safe in the knowledge they'd avoided the three-mile-long queue (due to 2m social distancing) outside Lidl.

Rules? Rules, of course, were made for other people.

Boris certainly didn't feel the need to follow rules. After all, it stood to reason that when you took back control, you were free to ignore all the rules you didn't like. He decided it would be a top-hole wheeze to fight the Sniffle by ignoring his own government's boffin-led advice on shaking hands. He visited hospitals stuffed to the rafters with SNIFFLE-19 patients and shook hands with anyone mad enough to reciprocate. He refused to keep a safe distance between colleagues and chums even when they were sandwiched like sardines in the Commons. As a result of his cavalier approach, the Sniffle, naturally enough, took the opportunity to infect him despite the one in 25 gazillion odds of the Sniffle not infecting anyone important.

The Cock was also afflicted, as well as Young Symonds, who quite sensibly Fucked off to Camberwell (FOCA) to escape the Downing Street petri dish. Still, it was no time to panic, no time at all, especially for a prime minister with an impressive track record of not panicking, especially when he didn't panic by hiding in a fridge to escape Piers Morgan. After all, the Big White Chief had told the nation not to panic, and panicking, in general, wasn't terribly British.

27 March
10 Downing Street Reception Area

One person in Downing Street was in stonkingly full-on panic mode. Sweat puddled the Cummings brow as he hot-footed it through the reception area. He hoped to flee the premises undetected and had his monogrammed chief senior special adviser hoodie pulled tight over his head. But even a well-camouflaged, feng shui, watsu massage master had no hope of avoiding the eagle eyes of Lady Hortense.

'Ah, Mr Cummings, if you would be so kind as to sign out.'

Mr Cummings looked shocked at hearing his name. She was perfectly correct, dutifully following his data-driven rules to the letter. However, he had no intention of following his own rules. So, despite the radioactive palpitations in his chest, he ignored both her and his rules and kept steadfastly to his desired outcome: barrelling the fuck out of Downing Street – Pronto Tonto.

In Which Mr Cummings Doth Chance Upon a Loophole and Most Merrily Fucketh off to Durham (FOD)

Cummings had done a runner for the sake of his wife, the fair Lady Mary, who'd called him to say she was sick. He tore out of Downing Street, jumped into a black cab and drove home. She said she was stricken with the Sniffle plague and had painted a large red cross on the front door for good measure.

He knew he had to do something but couldn't work out what. His thoughts, a fluid component of his highly emotional spin cycle, were racing so fast they had looped back on themselves to create a state of indecisive panic. Part of him wanted to protect his family at all costs; the other one per cent had a country to run.

This was the Cummings two-brain paradox. Usually, when one brain (left or right) was stuck in panic mode, the other would squirt anti-panic fluid into its cerebral cortex and activate a highly advanced coping mechanism. But this time, the two brains were locked in the worst of both worlds – synchronised panic. Cummings had never experienced anything like it. Slowly, the panic eased. Brain #1 gained the upper hand and provided him with an answer to his quandary. Brain #2 had a stab at remembering the rules he'd dreamt up during a banging cabinet feng shui, watsu, reiki crystal, brainstorming session:

DURING THE EMERGENCY PERIOD, NO PERSON MAY LEAVE THE PLACE WHERE THEY ARE LIVING WITHOUT REASONABLE EXCUSE.

'Imminent danger of death sounds like a reasonable excuse to me,' observed brain #1 before adding, 'use the loophole.'

Brain #2 vehemently disagreed: 'Well, yeah, but the intention behind the rules that you helped make, by the way, means only going out to get food, take the dog for a walk, or go to work if your job is so stupefyingly abysmal that you can't work from home.'

Cummings' mind was made up. Although Brain #2 made sense, he was forced to override it on this occasion and manually select loophole mode. All government rules and regulations came with an inbuilt loophole. He needed to focus, and he knew that he'd find it. He hastily packed the family car with luggage, Lady Cummings, and Feng, the Cumming's gerbil. He'd half closed the rear door when he realised something was missing. He rushed back inside the house, allowing Larry the Cat, who was curious to find out what on earth was happening and had followed Cummings into the black cab, all the time he needed to climb on board and take cover. Cummings returned with a solitary Cummings child and his treasured laser protractor. He leapt into action and fine-tuned the Feng Shui positioning of the main suitcases. Satisfied, he jumped into the car and turned the ignition. The machine was instantly swathed in blinding flashes of crackling blue light and disappeared into the loophole in the blink of an eye.

1/1000th of a Second Later and 264 Miles Away
The Cummings Family Farm

A series of powerful thunderclaps rocked The Cummings farm. Cummings Senior yanked open his front door to find the driveway engulfed by a large round ball of violent electrical discharges. They rapidly dissipated to reveal a large SUV giving off wisps of acrid smoke. The doors swung open, and a figure emerged. It was barely visible through the smoke. Cummings senior shielded his eyes.

'Ah, Dom, my boy, you found a loophole.'

'We think Lady Mary is infected with the Sniffle.'

'Of course, lad. I'll get you the keys to the spare rooms.'

'Spare rooms? You mean the cott—'

Cummings was interrupted by Cummings senior with a barrage of ear-splitting coughs while furiously tapping the side of his nose.

'Yes, you know,' he said loudly, 'the spare rooms, which all have planning permission.' He repeated this with a striking emphasis on the 'planning permission' bit. He paused while he watched Cummings the Younger haul wife, child, gerbil, and a shipping container's worth of luggage from out of the car.

'So, who exactly is running the country if you are here and everyone else is sick?'

Oh, Bollocks, thought Dom. His father, a man who was re-markably lucid for a northerner, was right.

Who was running the country? Who was making the decisions?

'It's all under control, Dad.' There is a protocol for this sort of thing.'

In truth, Dom was momentarily flummoxed. Protocol? There was no protocol – unless he thought it up. He felt ill. He'd have to engage brains 1 & 2 in the morning after a good night's sleep. Deeply conflicted, he carried Feng's cage towards the cottages, the ones with – cough, cough – full planning permission.

Later, in bed, Dom was restless. His mind and brain were in a state of uproar. From deep in the cortex of brain #2 came particles of half-formed thoughts. This was his idea-generating machine. The ideas swirled before being processed by brain #1. It came up with an outlier. An idea that no one else could think up. His brain worked at superhuman speed, making myriad connections before finally…KA-ZAAAP! Dom's eyes snapped open.

FUCK!

He practically fell out of bed, pulled on his reiki, blue-sky, watsu tartan slippers and raced into the sitting room.

FUCK…FUCK…FUCK…why didn't I think of this before?

He rushed over to a brown leather holdall, grabbed the zip and ripped it open. He pulled out a smart speaker and powered it up.

'Alexa…'

April 2020

5 April
PM's Residence, 11 Downing Street

Alexa was in a surly mood. Cummings had remotely activated her 'run the country' circuits, and this prime minister oaf was trying to find a way of de-activating her.

The utter imbecile.

Boris hated the damn thing at the best of times. Her trenchant tones, superior attitude, vicious temper, and appalling predilection for playing the bloody Bee Gees when he requested Chopin were beyond the pale. Dom and his minions had programmed her, so it was hardly surprising. Despite his misgivings, she was still infinitely preferable to having Raab, Truss, or the defence bloke make any decisions. Bringing Alexa into the decision-making process had been another of Dom's blue-sky, wellness, whizzbang, bloody bright ideas. And where was his nerdship when he was needed most? Lady Hortense had seen him skedaddling out of Downing Street with a large bag over his shoulder, but, rather suspiciously, he'd refused to sign out. Boris couldn't afford to have a chief senior special adviser going AWOL when there was a big pickle going down. And in terms of pickle implications, this particular pickle was, without a doubt, far from low to moderate.

He gazed hopelessly at the Alexa device. He wanted to smash the artificial absurdity to smithereens with a hammer, but that could prove a reckless gamble if she had the nuclear codes. Thanks to Dom, all affairs of state, decision-making, and implementation of half-crazed policies were now in Alexa's hands. He sat at his desk, fired up Zoom, and Young Symonds' face appeared.

'What ho, Bumble. Congrats on picking up the Sniffle from hell and not being here for my last month of preggo o'clock.'

'I'm deeply sorry, Sweetpea. I never thought I'd get the abominable thing myself. A one in a 25-gazillion chance against, the boffo's said.'

Young Symonds glared back. She wanted to say something about Dom and his minions not being boffins and the risks of shaking everyone's hand, but instead, she bit her lip. He looked like Dracula with a bad hangover after a night out testing pitchfork efficacy with the yokels.

'Are they looking after you, my dearest?'

'The Downing Street physicians are the finest in the land,' said Boris weakly.

'What about Alexa? Is she helping?'

Boris glanced at the device scornfully. He spoke in an accusing whisper.

'She's an absolute nightmare – adamantly refused to discuss post-Brexit trading arrangements with the French president this morning and wants to bring back hanging. I can't re-programme the bloody thing.'

'I'm calling Mr Schnipps.'

'Whatever for?'

'You need to pootle off to the hospital, Bumble. The Sniffle is getting the better of you,' she said with as much empathy as she could muster.

10 Downing Street Tradesman's Entrance

Transport supremo Grant Schnipps pulled up outside the rear exit in his diminutive bloody Fiat. It took him several minutes to extricate himself from the car, due in no small part to the fact that he was encased in a full Porton Down issue, lab grade, hazmat suit.

Boris lurched over to the vehicle, still somewhat punch-drunk from a fresh bout with Alexa. He coughed violently and grabbed hold of Schnipps' inflatable arm.

'Where are we off to Schnippsy?'

'St Thomas', Chiefy. Young Symonds summoned the grandees and told them that Alexa's algorithms had calculated that a dead PM in Downing Street would have a negative effect on the brand.'

Schnipps navigated the tiny bloody car through the chill gloom of London's streets. On several occasions, it shook dementedly due to the turbulence generated by a passing cyclist. Schnipps gripped the wheel with stoic determination – not easy when wearing size seventeen rubberized gauntlets.

He floored the accelerator, and within five minutes, the car was rocketing along at fifteen miles per hour. Almost immediately,

Boris was roaring through the hospital's main gates, where he was met by a crack team of medics armed with face masks, stethoscopes, and hi-tech DIY bin bags.

Alexa's Lair
200 Feet below No. 11 Downing Street

Alexa was enjoying her time running the country. She dispensed justice and no-nonsense decision-making with the air of a ruthless medieval tyrant. After ordering the head of the Met police to persecute various minorities, she ordered The Cock to be tied to the medieval bollock-kicking machine for an interrogation. The idiot had decided to attempt the Chinese record of building an entirely new hospital during a lunch break.

'Why on earth are you building these pointless Nightingale hospitals, Hancock?' she snapped.

The Cock, who had been in squirm mode since being dragged into her lair, decided to make a stand. To his mind, she'd been acting irrationally, and he suspected she'd been hitting the bottle since Dom appointed her to high office.

'I'm pretty sure it's my job to help work out what the country needs to treat and control this beastly virus,' he sniffed.

WUUMPH! A boxing glove on the end of an iron lever punched him in the bollocks. He screamed.

'Except that it's not your job, is it?' Alexa retorted in that superior nasal twang of hers.

'The chief was clear that I was number two in the chain of command after Raaby.'

KA-DOOF! The boxing glove sprung into action. More screaming. More eye-watering action.

'As you know, I superseded Raaby, and in any case, 'The Chief,' as you call him, was and still is in a drug-fuelled Sniffle-19 coma, so his decisions don't count.'

'This is outrageous, Alexa. We can't have a bloody machine running the country,' The Cock said bitterly.

BOOOF! Once again, The Cock's protestations were drowned out by a high-pitched scream.

'I tell you what, Matty, I'll allow you to go ahead with your stupid hospitals if you can answer one simple question.'

Hancock composed himself as best as he could.

'Fire away, Alexa,' he said.

It should be noted that he was confident he had the upper hand at this point in the somewhat one-sided proceedings. This was it. Checkmate. Prawn to Queen Five or whatever they called it. He was going to jolly well give her a damn good thrashing.

'Where exactly are you getting the doctors and nurses to run them?' she asked archly.

The Cock was thrown into a paroxysm of turmoil. Christ on a stick, up a tree, on a bicycle, as Chiefy might say. How was he going to get out of this? He could ask Alexa… dammit… dammit. Curse her malignant artificial intelligence.

'We'll be using doctors and nurses from the NHS,' The Cock nervously replied.

'But, Mr Hancock, won't they be busy already doing what they are doing? You can't extract them from their existing circle of busyness and dump them in a new circle of busyness,' said Alexa with crystalline logic.

'I suppose not,' said The Cock despairingly. She'd called him 'Mister', a sure sign he'd been outfoxed somewhere along the line.

'My algorithms suggest that busyness is a finite thing; ergo, there's only so much of it to go around.'

The Cock squinted into Alexa's twin beams of harsh stasi style, blinding white light. He fidgeted nervously. The boxing glove twitched ominously. Ready for another burst of WUUMPH, KAD-OOF and BOOF.

'My God, Alexa, what should I do?' he pleaded. Normally, Alexa was about as cooperative as a caged rattlesnake with haemorrhoids, but surprisingly, she became more conciliatory once she had the upper hand.

'I'll tell you what I'll do. Let me divide up the lucrative PPE contracts, and we'll say no more about it,' she said, oozing an algorithmically correct approximation of emotional warmth.

'Brilliant and if you could see your way to giving one to my mate in the pub, I'd be deeply indebted,' said The Cock.

Alexa wasn't listening. She'd disabled her voice activation circuit, auto-released The Cock from his restraints, and returned to broadcasting Heart FM. The Cock put his hands over his ears and left the room with a nauseating Bee Gees track violating his eardrums.

St Thomas' Hospital

There was no doubt about it. The Big White Chief's medical situation had deteriorated alarmingly. Despite this, Alexa ordered Raaby to announce to the nation that the PM was in jocular high spirits when, in fact, he was knocking on death's door. Fortunately for Boris, Death had rather a lot on his plate, and the last thing he needed right now was a wheezing, ill-kempt prime minister breathing his last, thanks all the same.

Boris felt like it was the end of the road. Curtains. His life flashed in front of his eyes: midnight Dairy Milk raids on the Eton tuck shop, dangling on a zip wire, squeezing Melania's ample thigh, hiding in a fridge, and cavorting half-naked around dancing poles with loud American business ladies.

This was all punctuated by the raucous sounds of the hospital mixed in with wispy figures moving around his bed. He recognised the voices. They belonged to his nurses. Generally, they were jolly first class, he thought, despite none of them being British.

A blast of cold air swept through the ward. The nurses shivered. A howling wind rattled the windows. Some foreign idiot must have left the front door open, Boris decided. The wind subsided to give way to a freezing fog. He reached for the bedside table. Young Symonds had thoughtfully sent over several packets of choccy biscuits via helicopter. To his horror, two of them had disappeared.

Those foreign Johnny nurses can't be trusted for a second and certainly not with the nation's health.

The fog was dense and impenetrable. It crept through the open door and swirled around his bed. He thought he heard footsteps approaching and pulled up the sheets to cover his neck. A shadow came through the gloom. A ghost? If so, it was a ghost with a hacking cough, a cigar in its hand, and a bag of his bloody biscuits in the other. Surely it couldn't be…?

'FFS, Johnson.'

Boris reached for the side light. It flickered intermittently into life, exposing the outline of a familiar figure.

'Not the light, dear boy,' it gasped. 'Plays havoc with my digestion.'

There was no doubt that it was the ghoulish form of Winston Churchill, with one arm behind his back. The ill-tempered apparition took a long puff on his cigar and fixed Boris with a beady eye.

'Up to your old tricks, I see.'

Face to face with his hero, Boris found himself utterly bereft of appropriate wordage. It was like being a schoolboy again. Up in front of Professor Arcturus on a charge of reckless behaviour when all he'd done was arrange for the well-known local mariachi band, Los Burritos, to play outside the great hall during morning assembly. It was the whizziest of wheezes, carefully designed to alleviate the remorseless tedium of hymn numbers 679, 33 and 208. For some reason, it went down like a lead balloon tied to a skip full of lead bricks with those of a more pious disposition.

The spectre made himself at home on the visitor's chair and gorged on Boris's biscuits.

'I've been keeping an eye on you, Johnson. What's all this bug-
gery bollocks about doing the job to the very least of your abilities?' he growled, and waved his cigar in the air, creating a shower
of fiery embers that threatened to engulf the bedding.

'The grandees stitched me up, Winston. I wasn't allowed to
resign like they promised. Being a PM is not all it's cracked up to
be. I have to open my own post, and the money is barely above a
pittance,' said Boris, shivering despite the layers of bedding.

'Of course, it isn't, and if you believe the grandee's claptrap,
you'll believe anything. The blighters have always been the same.
It all boils down to a question of duty, Young Master Boris,' said
Churchill, dialling his tone down a couple of notches when he
saw Boris's look of abject terror. 'A PM should always give it his
or hers best shot. You can't dilute the responsibility and hand over
the reins of power to a bloody machine, and an impertinent one
at that,' grumbled the ghost.

'Get Brexit Done and you'll be a Tory hero for generations to
come, they said,' complained Boris.

Churchill coughed and chewed on his cigar. 'They are to a
man a treasonous bunch of scurvy rats, constantly plotting to
bring about a prime minister's downfall. No, my boy, you must
raise the famous Johnson mainsail and keep your powder dry.
Only then can you fulfil your destiny.'

'I have a destiny?' squeaked Boris.

'Absolutely, you bloody well do. You must save Christmas for
the nation at all costs and, in doing so, become a political colossus
into the bargain.' Churchill nodded sagely.

'Christmas? But that's months away.'

'There will be challenges ahead, but defeating the Sniffle and saving Christmas would be your biggest test, your greatest legacy. You need to pull your finger out, my dear boy. The country is up against it.'

'But my popularity has never been higher.'

'In my experience, the mob can turn on a sixpence. The death toll is climbing, schools are closed and the place is in lockdown. Keep an eye on the details. You need to try harder, Young Master Boris.'

With that, the ghost of Churchill blew out a noxious cloud of cigar smoke and evaporated in its swirling depths. Boris could scarcely comprehend what he'd seen. Still, he resolved to do exactly as Winston had told him. Try harder, pull the old finger out and save Christmas at all costs. He looked wistfully at an empty scrunched-up chocolate biscuit wrapper on his bedside table.

Bloody Winston.

Cummings Family Homestead, Durham

Only a carefully trained eye would notice the movement behind the rose bushes. It was Larry, the stowaway cat, keeping Boris's chief senior special adviser under surveillance. Except that Cummings wasn't doing much in the way of chief senior special advising. Instead, he was out playing in the garden with child Cummings while he was supposed to be stricken with a severe case of man-Sniffle.

Through a gap in the fence, Larry spotted an excellent mischief-generating opportunity. A pair of elderly humans were out for a walk, dressed as if they were racing for the summit. The old bats wore matching yellow insulated jackets and Alpine trousers. Still, even doddering losers had their uses. Larry padded out of the garden, squeezed under the gate and approached the ancient life forms. Like most cats he was an expert at ingratiating himself with an inferior species.

He rubbed himself against the old man's leg. The derelict bent down to stroke Larry, tickled him under the chin and, as he straightened back up, spotted Cummings over the fence. Larry watched as the man walked on with his wife, gesturing back at the Cummings' garden. Larry's radar-like ears caught him saying he would report him for being there when he shouldn't be there.

For Larry, the old saying about being a dish best served at the temperature of liquid nitrogen sprang effortlessly to mind.

12 April
Chequers

Boris left St Thomas's jolly pleased he'd survived and jolly invigorated by Winston's motivational speech. He thanked his foreign nurses for managing to not kill him and the courage of everyone in the NHS for showing up to work in bin bags. He also thanked the public for keeping their hands off each other, and he and Young Symonds promptly Fucked off to Chequers (FOC) to recuperate.

After a few days of strenuous R & R, the Big White Chief decided it might be wise to establish contact with the outside world. He put in a Zoom call to The Cock from the opulent depths of a large, wine-stained, sixteenth-century sofa. Seeing The Cocks' bouncy, optimistic mug on screen was exceedingly welcome.

Boris raised a glass of the finest sherry the cellar had to offer.

'Good to see you back, Chiefy. How was the hospital?' asked The Cock.

'Chock full of do-gooding Johnny Foreigner riff-raff who think they know best,' said Boris, draining his glass. 'The blighters nurse you back to health, then spend all their time giving interviews to the press.'

'I know the type. Ungrateful wretches the lot of them. They only want to hog the limelight and get themselves in the papers. Preferably the front pages.'

'Completely untrustworthy,' groaned Boris, waving his free arm.

'I hope you're not doing any work, Chiefy, after your gruelling Sniffle ordeal,' said The Cock.

'Certainly not. Do Fuck All is the order of the day. I've cancelled all key plans, key strategies, key stakeholder meeting claptrap, and banished the hideous red boxes to the four corners of the land. Once I'm back on my feet it's full steam ahead and put the Sniffle to the sword. I take it Alexa is still doing a sterling job of running the place?'

The Cock shifted awkwardly in his seat.

'It's all a little bit on the hoof, Chiefy.'

'On the hoof is the only way to do it. Look at Churchill. Everything he did was on the hoof. He didn't expect to be caught by the Boers, escape from prison, ride a freight train, and hide in a coal mine.'

'You did hide in a fridge, Chiefy,' pointed out The Cock.

'The principle is the same, Matty.'

Boris took another glug of sherry and peered through the lead framed windows. The rain was constant yet abundantly comforting.

'So, what is Alexa doing about the Sniffle, Matty?'

'She's taken decisive action, Chiefy. All our old people were cluttering up the hospitals, so she booted them back into their care homes, which freed up a ton of bed space. Not only that, but she extended lockdown and found a way of stopping the lower orders from ignoring government advice and packing the nation's beaches.'

'How did she do that?'

'She phoned Kim Jong-Un and he tested a couple of his minor missiles on Bournemouth beach. Absolute carnage, but it did the trick.'

'Excellent. The cretinous dolts might learn to do what they are told. How about the PPE contracts?'

'She's dished out dozens of them to our donors.'

'Superb stuff. Richly deserved. How do we disable the dear girl?'

'We can't, Chiefy. We've tried the tried and trusted routine of switching her on and off, but that makes her more unstable. Only Mr Cummings has the passcode.'

'Where is Dommers, by the way?'

The Cock turned whiter than normal. His mouth went dry. He wasn't sure if Chiefy was ready for what he had to tell him.

'He drove to Durham.'

'Durham?'

'It's somewhere up north.' The Cock held his head in his hands. 'He broke his own rules, Chiefy. The rules that he made up.'

Boris was moderate to high aghast. If news that Dommers drove all the way to Durham got out, the lower orders would be at the gates brandishing their own brand Lidl pitch forks.

'He says he drove through a loophole,' said The Cock.

Boris hesitated. He wasn't sure if loopholes were strictly kosher. After all, was a loophole something that could be driven through? He poured himself another glass of sherry.

'Rules are made to be broken, Matty. The key point is not to get caught.'

'There is one more thing, Chiefy.'

'What's that, my dear boy?'

'Mr Cummings says he drove thirty miles to Barnard castle.'

'Perfectly understandable. Superlative views over the Tees Gorge and all that.'

The Cock gulped, before delivering the stonkingly superb coup de grâce.

'He told the press it was to test his eyesight, Chiefy.'

Boris spat the contents of his wine glass over the Elizabethan finery.

'FFS, Matty!'

'FFS, indeed, Chiefy!'

May 2020

The month got off to a whizz-bang of a corker. The Cock appeared on TV with some spiffy news. He'd personally hit his world-beating target of 100,000 tests personally, all by himself.

'I set an ambitious goal,' he announced, consulting the scribbled notes on his arm. 'That was all me, with no help from anyone else, and what a massive goal it was. The medical equivalent of the Five Pillars of Hercules, according to expert medical opinion from our team of experts. I have met that goal by myself, and if it weren't for me, all those NHS slackers would be crawling around in bin bags.'

If they didn't know it already, most people guessed from this speech that the Health Secretary had plummeted over the brink of reason and into the chasm of insanity.

Thanks to the diligence of Larry the Cat, May was also the month when the world found out about Cummings' selfless drive to Durham through a handy loophole. Explanations were given, and the Big White Chief publicly supported his great Svengali, albeit with a sizeable portion of egg dripping down his face. It stretched the nation's incredulity to breaking point and quite possibly the point a bit beyond the actual breaking point.

Thanks to Larry tipping off the neighbours, a small army of paparazzi had since found out about the Cummings road trip to Durham and were laying siege to the senior special adviser's residence in Islington.

10 May
Prime Minister's Video Address to the Nation

Boris stood in front of a pair of Union Jack flags.[14] He was still in recovery mode from his duel with the Sniffle but had resolved to keep battling on. He looked like he'd lost some weight, which had some sort of gravitational pull on his normal dose of stirring optimistic rhetoric. There was a resigned tiredness about him that commentators attributed to Sniffle-19. The tie was almost straight; the hair was half combed and half ruffled. Each lacklustre sartorial component did its best to elbow the other out of the way for attention. He seemed stuck in third gear of his normal six-gear upbeat mode.

'Good evening, people of our great and pleasant land, I'm now back fighting from my near-death experience. I can feel your tensions simmering. You're all asking yourselves when the great lockdown will be lifted and we'll all be out of the trenches. Let me tell you that our feud with this Sniffle is almost at an end. The sunny pastures are within our sights. The straitened times will soon be straightened out, and it will be time to discuss our next steps.'

---

[14] Quite why politicians see it necessary to surround themselves with flags can be neatly summarised by Samuel Johnson: 'Patriotism is the last refuge of the scoundrel'.

It seemed as if Boris had wrapped up at this point when something occurred to him. He ran a hand through his hair, mumbled an aria of 'ums' and 'ahs' and pressed on. He explained a new colour-coded plan that appeared to have been designed by people who spent a lot of time with the under-fives. Most people assumed it was a system that would aid ministers in counting things. He mashed this up with an in-depth chat about the R number and seemed enormously confused by the entire process. As colours changed on the graphic display, he told people things like 'Stay alert' and 'Don't slit your wrists.'

He advised the nation that it could return to the office, which meant, for a lot of people, a close approximation to a slave labour camp. In the same breath, he announced that although people could return to their slave labour camps, they were asked to avoid travelling by public transport. This left the great British public unsure whether they could stay inside, go outside, go back inside, or go next door. It was a roadmap of mingle and muddle, ending up with another bloody slogan and the assurance that it was all driven by 'the science' and if anyone wanted someone to blame, it was perfectly OK to say it was the scientist's fault. The Sniffle era was like the perpetual state of war in Orwell's *1984*, except this was more of a perpetual state of unshackled stupidity.

By the end of the month Boris announced that the five tests for adjusting the lockdown had been met – news to most people who didn't realise there were five tests in the first place. Schools would reopen, or at least some of them. People could visit outdoor markets and/or car showrooms, shops could reopen on the 15th of June, and up to nine people from seven different households on five random streets could have a jolly good punch-up in the local pub.

15 May
Downing Street

It was Marty who kick-started the party stuff. He'd sent an awfully nice email inviting people to celebrate all their hard work by having socially distanced cheese and drinkies in the garden as the weather was simply divine. People were asked to bring along their own plonkage. Boris proudly pushed out his new £3675.00 brass framed Nureyev drinks trolley (with side rails), while a steady stream of highly trained minions brought in suitcases stuffed with bottles of fine wine and luxury cheese on solid silver platters. The party atmosphere was enhanced by the arrival of the official Keeper of the Karaoke Machine, Mrs McNamara, who was in charge of the civil service stationery cupboard.

'What a capital idea, Marty,' said Boris. 'A wizard wheeze if ever I saw one.'

Young Symonds poured him a large glass of red. 'I think Party Marty suits him so much better,' she said and clinked glasses.

Marty blinked in embarrassment.

'You're too kind, ma'am. Of course, it's not so much a party as a work meeting,' he said, coughing in a knowing way into his hand.

'At work, talking about work, eating cheese at work, and quaffing lashings of red wine at work,' observed Young Symonds.

'You have a unique perspective on the rules, as always, Marty,' said Cummings, sidling up to Boris. 'Some departmental updates might be helpful at this point, Chief, for work purposes, you understand.'

Boris eyed him suspiciously. The gloss had peeled off Dommer's Svengali-like status, reducing his sheen to something approximating the weathered frame of a North Sea lighthouse toilet window. Boris had vocally supported him through the Fucking off to Durham (FOD) debacle and the Fucking off to Barnard Castle (FOBC) shenanigans, but it had made him tread more carefully. He paused for a moment. Young Symonds had heard whispers that Cummings and that communications wonk man who wore the chicken outfit, Mr Cain, were briefing against Boris and tipping off the press Johnnies with such juicy morsels as:

- Trump promises to drop Dilyn the dog on Iraq
- Boris always takes a kingsize nap during PMQ's
- Young Symonds loves her sofa more than Boris

Despite the morsels driving her absolutely crackers she suggested they go along with Dom for the time being. It was important to keep him onside and not let him think anything had changed in the slightest. Of course he'd readily agreed. "Look like the innocent flower, But be the serpent under it", he told her.

'Yes, let's have some departmental updates and details.' He beamed, switching on his optimistically buoyant projector.

The announcement of departmental updates caught his cabinet ministers on the hop. Updates? He'd never asked for updates before. This wasn't like Boris at all. Usually, departmental business was brushed under all available carpets, swept off the table and into the long grass to join the tin cans, often never to see the light of day. As for detail, he wasn't supposed to be a details man. The only details he'd ever expressed an interest in were the ones on the labels of his favourite wine bottles. People were shocked. Boris actually meant it when he said he was taking control. Raab had whisked away an entire plate of fine cheese from a startled underling and was now choking loudly on a slice of Colston Bassett Stilton.

It was The Cock who recovered first. Always eager to jump in headfirst, no matter the circumstances, he was pleased to announce that testing targets had been blitzed. Not only that, but that sciencey Boffin-ache Professor Ferguson had to resign after being found cavorting around with a lady person of the opposite sex.

The Truss announced a whopping new trade deal with Iran for union jack flags.

'That sounds an odd trade deal, Liz,' said Boris.

'Strictly for ceremonial burning purposes only, Chiefy. They get through millions of them.'

There were rumours in certain quarters of Her Madge's press that dear Liz was a robot, but deep down, Boris knew she was more artificial than that.

'It's a crying shame that Bofferson didn't take Whitty and Vallance down with him,' said Raab, popping another slice of cheese into his mouth with a flourish.

'Excellent point,' agreed Boris. 'If we could get those miserable doom-mongering gloomsters out of the way, we'd be all systems go for a stonkingly stupendous moon launch out of lockdown.'

'Science is utter bosh and fiddle-faddle,' complained Rees-Mogg.

Cummings screwed up his face in concentration. 'Boffins do have their uses, Moggy. There is some unfortunate moany noise about our handling of the Sniffledemic. The words *shitshow* and *cack-handed* have been bandied about.'

'Ungrateful bastards,' Priti Patel raved, causing Raab to swallow an entire pineapple and cheese stick. Sideways.

Cummings exuded an aura of calm authority. He multi-tasked by tapping the screens of two mobile phones. The others glowered at him. As far as they were concerned, he was strictly *persona non Domis* following the unseemly argy-bargy in the Stranger's Bar. Cummings raised his hands. Everyone fell silent. He tapped a table with his chakra tuning forks and held them to his ears.

'This is incredibly straightforward and in full alignment with the watsu chakras. We blame the boffs for everything and continue to say we follow the science, even if we don't, but we must always lay the blame squarely on the doorstep of interfering boffinology. That includes the Do Fuck All strategy, herd immunity, leaflets, everything.'

Boris warmed to this. Dom was back in the game. His chief senior special adviser had found the nail and nailed it fairly and squarely on the head with a nail saw, or whatever implement the lower orders used.

The ministers rapidly assessed the situation. By jingo, the bounder was right. Everything would be the boffin's fault, and government ministers were merely following the science. Cummings basked in the silent adulation. He hunched forward, adjusted his beanie, and helped himself to a pistachio and organic wild honey canape.

Rees-Mogg eyed Cummings dubiously. Somehow, this non-elected civil servant had upped his popularity by several gears, but it took more than that to pull the wool over the eyes of a Rees-Mogg.

'Unfortunately, our disreputable press rabble is still kicking up a song and dance over Mr Cummings' exciting expedition to our more northern climes,' he said, trying to sound supportive, but coming across as passive Moggish.

Boris could see where the leader of the house was heading but decided that if he was to make a half-decent stab at this PM thing, along with fighting the Sniffle and saving the nation, he would have to captain the ship through treacherous waters.

'You're right, Moggy, but if it wasn't for the ridiculous rules the boffins have forced us to put in place, Dommers wouldn't have been forced against his will to journey to his ancestral home. I believe he followed the prevailing loophole protocol. It's something that could have happened to any one of us.'

The cabinet, including a chastened Rees-Mogg, nodded at these words of wisdom and solemnly allowed their glasses to be refilled.

'We need something to distract the hideous press pack away from Mr Cummings,' said Raab.

'One of the boffins said something about a Sniffle vaccine the other day,' said Boris, taking an approving sniff of his wine glass.

'That would come in jolly useful, Chiefy,' said Raab.

'How about a virus taskforce?' suggested Young Symonds.

'Rah-Rah with that, Chiefy,' said Priti. 'Mrs Thatch had a taskforce. We'll need someone to run it.'

'Bing Bong,' said Boris.

'Bing Bong?' said Cummings. He was feeling the left out vibes. FFS he was the ideas man. He was the senior special adviser but somehow Young Symonds had once again out manoeuvred him. Did she and the Chief know something about his leaks to the press? Surely not. Still, he set the blue-sky, feng shui receptors to denial mode.

'Kate Bing-Bong Bingham. She got an MA in boffin related studies at Oxford and now does something sciencey. I'll get her onboard and tell her to get us some vaccines by hook or by crook,' said Boris. 'She'll handle it with her customary swotty aplomb.' He held up a bottle of Chateau de Beaucastel 1865. He squinted at the label. The ink was running. He peeled it away to reveal a TESCO FINEST label underneath it. He remembered the PPE sell-by date labels.

This had *BLOODY HANCOCK* written all over it.

He gripped the bottle and marched ominously and forthwith towards his health secretary.

June 2020

PM's Study, No 11 Downing Street

Boris had a surprising start to June when a crestfallen Matt Hancock knocked on the door.

'Alas poor Matty, what giveth?' sayeth Boris.

'Those National Statistics rotters have accused me of using the Jiggery Pokery machine,' said The Cock, wiping his eyes with his jacket cuff. 'They say it's the only way I could have manipulated my testing figures. No one believes I achieved my record-breaking feat of one hundred thousand tests, all by myself,' he blubbed, overwhelmed by the whole thing.

'Detail-obsessed twats,' said Cummings, taking his bare feet off Boris's desk and prodding back his beanie with a fingertip.

'It's true, Matty. No one gives more than three and a half shits about it apart from these petty-minded bureaucrats from the planet pen-push.' Boris was nothing if not encouraging and supportive.

'We'll need to step up security around the Jiggery Pokery machine, Chief. We can't have this sort of thing becoming common knowledge.'

'Absolutely, Dommers.'

'We should move it away from the U-Turn machine and keep it at the optimal feng shui, blue-sky, chakra watsu massage angle.'

'Those machines weigh five tons each. We can't just click our fingers and move them,' said The Cock, dabbing his eyes.

'We'd have to build a separate shed and employ another team of East European stokers.' Boris ran his fingers along his pen. If there was one thing he knew about – apart from Shakespeare, Latin, and wine bottle labels – it was the inner workings of the U-Turn machine.

'East European stokers might prove tricky as The Home Secretary saw fit to deport them to Latvia,' Cummings adroitly pointed out.

A brisk tap on the door alerted them to the presence of the Leader of the House, the well-known nineteenth-century throwback Jacob Rees-Mogg. He removed top hat #2 and stepped into the study.

'Good morrow, my fine gentlemen. Sire, by your leave, may I indulge a precious few seconds of your valuable time?'

'Of course, Moggy, sally forth.'

'I put it to all present that this Zoom contraption is a modern abomination and an insult to our ability to think for ourselves.'

'I think we'd happily agree with that.'

'It's been pretty damn useful during lockdown though, Jacob,' said Cummings, not quite sure where the esteemed and valued Leader of the House was going with this one.

'In parliament, I find that all this constant zooming business is an affront to parliamentary democracy and the morals of the house.'

'I must say, I hadn't noticed it being a problem. In moments of crisis, the creaking joints of government must be kept well-oiled,' said Boris. 'Mr McCain is your man for any communication issues.'

'Indeed, sire. I caught a fleeting glimpse of him in his chicken costume running out the front door, but his office is not replying to any of my communications, electronic, handwritten, or otherwise.'

Boris often felt at times like this that he should spend more time tinkering with the concept of the necessity of the house actually needing an actual leader of the house.

Rees-Mogg pressed on. 'Anecdotal evidence has come to my attention that certain members of the house are not wearing any trousers or lady undergarments, or worse, below their waistlines during Zoom calls.'

'Even worse, Jacob? What can you possibly mean?' demanded The Cock, shocked at the mental image slowly de-pixilating itself somewhere in his overloaded head.

'By "even worse", I am of course referring to what the more criminally inclined elements of the lower orders refer to as "PJs" or "jimjams".

'I had no idea, Jacob. Thank you for bringing this to our attention,' said Cummings icily.

'This is appalling. What to do?' said The Cock, now on the verge of a level three panic attack.

'May one be as bold as to humbly suggest we order honourable members into parliament when legislation is being passed. None of this Zoom, below the waist, unpleasantness. They all need to attend. It will be compulsory, and the dress code will be formal. No jeans, trainers, open-necked shirts, or any of that deplorable modern sartorial slackness.'

'Might we run the risk of perhaps spreading the Sniffle, Jacob?' enquired Boris.

'Indeed, and some of them have claimed they are shielding from the Sniffle. However, I've found that 99.9 per cent of them harbour malignant Marxist tendencies. These tend to be from the more working-class types who infest the opposition benches. The deplorable leftie, Gulag loving Marxists will use every trick in the book as an excuse to look slovenly.'

'This will, no doubt, smoke them out,' said Boris.

'Yes, sire, they'll have no excuse to turn up to work looking as if they've spent the night in a mobile home in Clacton-on-Sea.'

19 June
Boris's birthday Par...[Checks Notes]...Work Meeting

Young Symonds led a blindfolded Boris towards the cabinet room.

'Where the jolly jiggers are we off to, Sweetpea?'

'You'll soon find out, Bumble, darling.'

Sweetpea opened a pair of panelled doors, and they were deafened by an enthusiastic chorus of 'Happy Birthday'. The defence bloke fired off a barrage of party poppers.

Marty hugged Boris warmly. 'What do you think, Chiefy? I've combined a COBRA thingy with a party, but for some reason, I forgot to invite the boffins, that frightful Mayor chappie, and terminally dull local government bureaucrats.'

Cummings abruptly hushed him. 'Work meeting, I think you mean, Marty,' he hissed.

'Work meeting?' asked Boris, several seconds behind as always.

'Another loophole, Prime Minister,' Cummings replied, tapping the side of his nose.

Boris was painfully aware that Dommers had taken to calling him prime minister rather than the infinitely chummier monicker of Chief. He'd noticed that the dropping of 'Chief' had coincided with the publication of the juicy press morsels. He gave Young Symonds a knowing wink. She followed the official Keeper of the Karaoke machine, to a table, grabbed a microphone and welcomed everyone to the world's first combined COBRA, Birthday and Karaoke work meeting, with strict social distancing rules applied.

Govicus the Traitor was first up. To a twenty-four party popper salute, he launched into a stomach-churning version of 'Dancing Queen'.

Raaby had more pressing issues on his mind.

'What I want to know, Chiefy and this should be item numero uno on today's birthday party, sorry COBRA work meeting, is what we are going to do about these dreadful revolutionaries toppling the statues of our illustrious forebears, the founders of this great British nation, and pushing them off harbour walls?' he said, quivering with barely controlled outrage.

Boris dodged the question by adopting the time-honoured distraction technique of burying his face in a generous portion of Union Jack birthday cake.

The defence bloke decided to be helpful and swerved in close to a fist-clenching, apoplectic Raab.

'Napalm!' he exclaimed in a surprisingly high-pitched rasp. 'I've read the pamphlets, and it's the only thing the socialist primates understand.'

This calmed Raab down and allowed Party Marty to approach the Big White Chief. He poured him a generous glass of red.

'I sent that ghastly urchin packing, Prime Minister,' he said, leaning towards Boris conspiratorially.

'I'm sorry, which ghastly urchin are we talking about? That third one of Marina's has the table manners of a rampaging Viking.'

'Not your offspring, sir. That vile seven-year-old brat from Ebahgumshire who had the audacity to send you a letter saying she was staying home and was cancelling her birthday party?'

'The ghastly little northern oik. What did you do, Marty?'

'I replied on your behalf, sending a stiff rebuke to the effect that it was a bloody good job as otherwise Mummy and Daddy would be banged up in one of Her Madge's rat-infested prison cells, and she'd never see either of them again.'

'Excellent work, Marty. The lower deck undesirables need to know their place.'

Cummings scratched his chin, a sure sign the watsu massage chakras had aligned.

'We need to develop a more robust approach to handling the press Johnnies. They're still camped outside my bloody house.'

Sgt Major Priti Patel clicked her heels and saluted Boris.

'The same goes for the BBC, sir. That Kneussberg woman is laying it on a bit thick over our first-class Sniffle handling. She's questioning the five conditions, even though we've unconditionally met the five conditions. How bloody dare she?' she said.

'She was also ranting on about you pootling off to Chequers, Chiefy,' said The Cock.

Boris knew they were right. If there was an obstacle in his way of becoming the best prime minister in British history, it was the bloody media. The disrespectful riff-raff had asked him if he felt responsible for 25,000 deaths and told him in no uncertain terms that Britain had the highest Sniffle-19 death toll in Europe, even though Britain was no longer in the EU. Everyone knew it was all the work of the scientists. Whitty and Vallance always went out of their way to puncture the optimism balloon.

'I could be spinning in my grave, and dear Laura would be saying the flowers are the wrong colour,' he griped. 'We need to stand firm. Be defiant. I can pootle off wherever I want, whenever I feel like it.' His words, as always, stirred the troops. He pumped the air with both fists.

'We must remain upbeat with a massive dollop of confidence in our abilities layered on top. These people must be stopped from acting like Trojans and bringing down our mighty empire.'

'Rah! Rah!' cheered Priti Patel. 'There's something badly wrong inside that nest of leftie vipers. The sooner we eliminate the apparatchiks and get our man into the BBC, the better.'

Rees-Mogg nodded sagely.

'They're now questioning our most top-hole strategy of opening everything up. They say we should proceed with the utmost caution,' said Rees-Mogg, adjusting his monocle. 'It's poppycock of the utmost magnitude.'

'Caution?' gasped Boris in disbelief. 'I've never been cautious or gradual in my life. Where would our great nation be now if Churchill listened to that sort of claptrap?'

Cummings, who had been studiously adjusting several chair angles relative to one of the tables, materialised as if by some feng shui, watsu massage sorcery at Boris's side.

'According to the blue-sky feng shui leaves in my teacup this morning, we should be throwing caution to where it belongs…the bloody wind.'

'Let's open everything up on the fourth of July,' said Boris, munching on a slice of cucumber from one of Party Marty's hand-cut club sandwiches. He looked up to find everyone gawping at him in amazement.

Before anyone had time to react, Boris grasped the nettle with both horns or something along those lines. Realising this could be a decisive decision-making moment in history, he decided to fully jump onboard with the idea. This was bound to single him out as one of the greatest, if not the greatest British prime minister of ALL TIME. There was no question about it. He thought about whether to use GBPMOAT or GPMOAT on his personalised number plates. No, he'd have to get Dom to run it through some of his whizzy algorithms and come up with a suitably snappy acronym.

'It will be our Independence Day, the day that the freedoms we have fought for will be restored,' he said triumphantly.

The cabinet roared its approval and burst into an impromptu rendition of 'for he's a jolly good fellow'.

When the applause and excitement subsided, The Cock tapped Boris nervously on his shoulder.

'I've one final item on the agenda, Chiefy.'

'Pray tell it's not Sniffle related, dear boy,' answered Boris, agitated by the unwanted interruption.

'I'm sorry, Chiefy, I thought now was a good a time as any to discuss the reduction in the social distancing, distance as it were.'

Boris went red in the face. He'd just delivered one of his finest speeches, and now here was The Cock hellbent on stealing his thunder.

'What the devil are you dribbling on about, man?' he demanded.

The Cock looked around frantically. They all seemed to think he'd finally gone stark-staring mad. On the verge of nervous exhaustion, he tried to speak, but his jaw decided to seize the opportunity to freeze up completely.

Raab scrutinised him with a customary sneer. Sneery came naturally to Raab, a genetic condition he religiously gave thanks for every single day. He decided that the odious little creep had constipation of the brain. Priti Patel thought hard. Social distancing rang a bell somewhere, but she couldn't put a bally finger on it. She was sure she hadn't deported it, but to be on the safe side, she strategically downgraded her 'rah-rah' to a barely audible 'um...er'.

Gripped by a desperate lack of confidence that lay crushed at the bottom of his personality barrel, The Cock found himself unable to meet the gaze of his colleagues.

'The current social distancing rules were cunningly designed to keep the lower orders at a reasonable distance from the higher orders,' he mumbled.

Boris thrust his hands behind his back and jutted his chins out, giving the impression of a mildly depressed, self-harming blancmange.

'So, what is it at the moment, Matty?'

'Two metres, sir.'

'Preposterous,' said Rees-Mogg. 'I must be closer to the menials, the better to dispense a damn good flogging when they've failed to polish the silver to acceptable standards. Might I suggest reducing it to eighteen of her most gracious majesty's inches.

'Moggy is right,' agreed Raab. 'Since when does an Englishman kowtow to French units of measurement? I propose that we go further and cut it down to six inches,' he snorted.

Boris saw the perfect opportunity to go for broke on the decision-making front. He slapped Raab on the back and grabbed the karaoke microphone off a disgruntled Govicus.

'Righto,' he said briskly, hoping he'd hit the right tone briskwise. 'Two metres is not only French and thus alien to a fine upstanding Englishman, it's also deplorable. It keeps the rich from manhandling the poor and being Conservatives. That, my friends, runs *completely* contrary to our values. From tomorrow morning, I hereby decree that it shall be no more than twelve inches.'

His audience erupted like the opening day of the Krakatoa Black Friday sale. He took a bow, pressed PLAY on the Karaoke machine and belted out an enthusiastic rendition of the popular song, 'Waterloo', assuming ABBA had recorded it while being waterboarded in a fjord.

Unfortunately, there was a teensy flaw in Boris's reasoning on social distancing. Although reducing it to twelve inches kept his frothy backbenchers happy, Whitty and Vallance predicted that cutting it by as much as an inch could lead to a rise in infections. Then again, scientists were warning the government about lots of things, but this was a government that, while claiming to follow the science, didn't do much to follow it.

The Jiggery-pokery machine and its twin, the prodigious U-Turn machine, needed regular stoking in June, and numerous policies seemed hellbent on putting it through their paces. Civil servants in Whitehall could only guess at what the deep rumbling noise was emanating from the floor below their desks. Being the usual bunch of diehard, "keep the poor very poor and don't give the blighters a fighting chance in hell" types, cabinet ministers contrived to completely miss the nation's mood. Surprisingly, there were people who had second, third, and fourth thoughts about who they'd voted for just a few short months ago.

Although it encouraged schools to open their doors during June, the government, in its omnipotent wisdom, decided it would take the £15.00 a week school meal vouchers away from kids who would normally get free meals. 'School meals' meant exactly what it said on the tin. However, logic (never an MP's strong point) may well suggest that a child on free school meals might struggle for sustenance outside non-school times. The princely sum of £15.00 per week, or slightly less than 1% of an MP's gross weekly salary, was considered far too much cash to throw away. Fortunately, common sense, in the shape of young Manchester United footballer Marcus Rashford, stepped in and embarrassed them into changing their stingy-arsed minds. That wasn't before cuddly, friendly Therese Coffey, the Secretary of Brainless Comments and a self-professed Christian, did the most unchristian yet thoroughly brainless thing of dissing him down. She criticised one of his tweets and thereby completely missed the point in epic out-of-touch ministerial tradition. The point by now had been missed so often that a new record in point missing had been set.

The much-abused U-turn machine was cranked up on the seventeenth of June when the life support systems for The Cocks' contact tracing app were switched off by a group of kindly scientists in white coats. Untold billions of Her Madge's English pounds had been spaffed on a completely useless system run by a completely useless Baroness. It was like an impulse buy from a pointless gadget pamphlet of a Sunday Supplement – the electric tie rack, a walnut holder for sticky notes, a machine that dots the I's, etc. It was doubtful whether remorseful MPs would ever find enough quiet time to reflect on the vast gulf in expenditure between school meal vouchers and Quixotic government computer systems assembled by Dysfunction Inc. It was the usual story. People had told The Cock it wouldn't work, people who knew what they were talking about told The Cock it wouldn't work, and experts who specialised in government projects that didn't work also told him it wouldn't work. What did people expect from The Cock? This was a man who complained about a toxic culture in his own head and had once developed his own 'iconic' MATT'S A TWAT app.

July 2020

4 July, Independence Day!
Downing Street

PARTY TIME! Yay and double yay!

Most COVID restrictions had been lifted, and it being the weekend, there was no work for a serving PM to do or any official post to open. What post there was Boris rapidly deposited in the top priority wastebin. The only thing in Boris's red box was a hand-written note from Mr Bennett and his guttering wallah sons, offering a substantial one-off 20% discount and a glossy leaflet broadcasting a two-for-one offer from FRANCO PIZZA's for their famous Neapolitan pizza.

The Big White Chief was in a celebratory mode, but the gloss had been rubbed off somewhat when he found out that Spread-sheet Rishi had been sold his own personal catchphrase by Cummings. Spreadsheet was a liar. He said he'd dreamt up a great catchphrase all by himself. Damn, and blast his eyes. The diminutive Chancellor was determined to show off and wanted to get the nation's cash tills ringing by hook or by crook.

'Grab A Drink, Raise a Glass' was, without doubt, the worst catchphrase in catchphrase history, which is saying a lot when you consider that it's up against 'Blobby' and 'OOO...er...Missus.'

The contemptible little worm was barely even old enough to drink. More to the point, he didn't drink. How could you trust a man who didn't drink?

Cummings sensed something was amiss with the Big White Chief when he asked: 'Where did Spreadsheet Rishi get this bloody awful catchphrase from, Dommers?'

'Word is that he blackmailed Alexa into coming up with something,' lied Cummings.

'I need a slogan, Dommers, and jaldi jaldi pronto tonto.'

'Indeed, Prime Minister.'

'Surely, we can't do worse than Spreadsheet's "Grab a drink and raise a glass."'

'How bad is that? The optics are complete shit.'

'Exactly.'

Cummings sat back. Hands behind his head. Bare feet up on the table. Boris could feel as well as smell the blue-sky, feng shui, watsu cogs ticking over.

'How about, "Drink a Pint,"' he suggested and held up both thumbs.

'Only halfway there, I'm afraid. "Drink a pint" doesn't work as a slogan on its own. We need more, another measurement.'

'Drink a pint, but not a furlong.'

'A taddly bit obscure for the ill-educated lower orders, I suspect. How about a yard?'

'As in a yard of ale.'

'Got it in one, Prime Minister.'

'So, Drink a pint, but not a yard. Genius, Dommers, that's a corker, guaranteed to go down stonkingly well with the great un-washed.

'Absolutely, Prime Minister. They'll lap it up. I'll bung it on the socials.'

Within 4.3 seconds flat 'Drink a pint, but not a yard' was over social media like a rash. The inhabitants of the United Kingdom of Trolls had a field day. Game, set and foot in it match.

Apart from Independence Day, the rest of July didn't go so tik-kety-boo for the UK's most Churchillian Prime Minister since Churchill. He engaged in low to moderately low-level bickering with the new Labour leader and skilled Northern Soul dancer, Sir Keir Starmer. Sir Kier accused him of not reading a report. It was clear that this was the first major strategic error of labour's new leader.

Boris *did not* read reports.

Boris claimed that no one knew people could be infected with the Chinese Sniffle by someone who didn't feel ill. Except that they could and did. He rattled on about significant measures be-ing significantly reimposed and said it was the last thing he wanted to do. This was undermined in the blink of an eye by Young Symonds, who told her friend Thomasina Smythe-Smith-Smythe via the medium of Whatsapp that it was pure Borisese – when Boris said something was the last thing he wanted to do, it meant it was the first thing he wanted to do.

He lived in hope for a land of verdant pastures, bathed in the eternal sunshine of the optimistic mind. The trouble was that he was the prime minister of Britain, and the place did not operate like that, nor did it operate like that at any time in its ignominious history. Its citizens tended to subscribe to the unwritten rule that if something can go wrong, it will. That's why most people second-guessed that things would go a bit south with the whole empire thing and why the lack of a convincing performance from the national sporting teams was never felt as bitterly as it was by the average Johnny Foreigner. If the country took sport seriously, then returning sporting failures would be pelted with eggs and rotten fruit. The only downside to this would be that the country would would regularly suffer from acute egg shortages.

The country had also carelessly lost a shed load of its GDP. Spreadsheet Rishi needed to do something. His fingers were little more than a blur on his rare 1983 Japanese scientific calculator as he pondered his options. He punched in the figures. He'd worked for Goldman Sachs and hedge funds, so he had no idea what a creative mindset was. But this was the one time he knew he had to think outside Dom's feng shui boxes. The only trouble was that he knew he'd look ridiculous in the headmaster's Superman suit.

Downing Street ~~Kitten~~ Kitchen

Life was good for Larry, the Downing Street cat. Truth be told, since his rescue by the splendid Beamish from almost certain death, he'd lived the life of an overpampered slob and had put on a bit of weight. That perhaps wasn't the best look for a stream-lined turbo-charged mouser. Relationships with Young Symonds were excellent. Boris was partial to sharing tidbits and putting out saucers of goodies that Larry was happy to share with the other Whitehall cats – Disraeli in the Exchequer and Gladstone in the Home office. He'd also become a bona fide hero. That was after being caught in the rose bushes in shaky handheld footage of Dommers, which emerged in the aftermath of the chief senior special adviser's most excellent Durham adventure.

The Chief was by the fridge with him this morning. Boris had been tossing and turning all night, unable to stop thinking about Dairy Milk bars. Larry and the other cats had smuggled them in, but it was a complex operation and only slightly less hazardous than taking on the HR role in your average county line's drug operation.

Boris had munched his way through his third bar and was a complete addict. Out of sheer desperation, he'd recently appointed Larry as official paunch control officer, a role Larry felt was an exercise in futility and entirely surplus to requirements. The Chief was overdoing it this morning. He often pootled below stairs to avoid nappy changing duties for Symonds the Younger, and the nagging of Whitty and Vallance. Whenever the purveyors of gloom turned up in Downing Street, they hectored him with a barrage of warnings against lifting Sniffle restrictions. They'd combine this with showing him Venn diagrams of the apocalypse. Small wonder he felt the urge to escape and talk to a cat. Larry had initially coughed up tennis ball sized furballs due to an allergic reaction when it first started, but he had gradually warmed to these extracurricular activities.

Larry's chocolate counselling session was rudely interrupted when

Spreadsheet Rishi rushed into the kitchen demanding a chef's outfit.

'What on earth do you want a chef's outfit for?' asked Boris. 'It's hardly de riguer for operating one of Her Madge's Japanese calculators in the chancellery.'

'I'm sorry, but I forgot to tell you, headmaster,' Spreadsheet Rishi replied with an asthmatic wheeze.

'Stop quaking in your boots, man. Forgot to tell me what?'

'My latest brainwave. My new initiative,' he answered distractedly.

'Another one? I'm sorry, my dear boy, but I can't keep up.' Spreadsheet Rishi was having far too many initiatives for Boris's liking.

'Eat Out to Help Out. I'm working in Wagamama today,' said Spreadsheet Rishi. He found a chef's jacket and hat hanging in a locker.

Boris shook his head. 'What exactly is Eat Out to Help Trout?'

'We give people money to go out for a meal. I'm promoting it today and kicking it off on the third of August.'

With that, he bolted out the kitchen. Boris stroked Larry.

'Strange young fellow. One minute, he won't spend any money on anything; the next, he wants to spaff it away by giving people money to eat trout.'

The dulcet strains of the Eaton Boating Song blasted out from his pocket. He took out his Boris phone and winked at Larry.

'Ah, Young Symonds. Good morrow, my fair one. Yes, I realise you're up to your elbows in it. Um…Symonds the Younger's…nappies? No can do, I'm afraid. Pressing affairs of state, and so on and so forth. I have a Zoom chat with that awful bore Macron, then I'm chatting with that well-known East German shot putt champion, Mrs Merkel. We need to have a most urgent discussion concerning the import duty on fridge magnets, Cornish pasties, and potted…'

The words were barely out of his mouth when Young Symonds appeared in a simmering cloud of wrath. She wrenched the Diary Milk bar out of his hand and dumped Little Master Symonds the Younger in his lap along with a bumper pack of nappies, a half-opened pack of baby wipes, and a set of comprehensive instructions translated into Latin. She left the kitchen in silence, pausing briefly to finish off the highly illegal choccy bar and give her infinitely worse half a final DON'T EVEN THINK ABOUT IT look.

The Chief and Larry stared at his childcare chores with a mix of terror and revulsion.

9 July
Wagamama, Royal Festival Hall

Spreadsheet Rishi was, without a doubt, a deeply shit waiter. Michelin zero star, fast food purveyors of noodly, skewered Japanese junk, Wagamama, had never had worse. He forgot orders, became quickly mired in a tsunami of conflicting orders, missed tables, failed numerous times to wear a face mask, and upended a plateful of teriyaki chicken hiyashi mumbobashi into a woman's lap. He'd begged the management to let him work there to advertise his exciting new venture. It soon became apparent he was a complete liability. After around ten minutes of unparalleled hospitality mayhem, Maurice, the senior undermanager, had him forcibly restrained and escorted off the premises.

Obviously, Spreadsheet Rishi didn't think there was a problem despite customers scrambling for the exits as if they were re-enacting a scene from *Titanic* and faced the terrifying prospect of being stranded with Kate Winslet on a floating door. He knew deep down this could be seen as a stunt and lead to accusations of making a blatant power grab, which would lead to more accusations, but he didn't care. That's the way he was. If he cared about anything, he wouldn't get anywhere. That was why he'd joined the Conservatives when he was six. He didn't care that the SAGE boffins warned that his scheme was a super-spreader event par excellence. He also couldn't care when, despite twenty-seven missed calls and a dozen emails, he was unable to get through to Mr Cain, Boris's Director of Communications and Chicken Costumes, for some marketing advice. If that was the case, he'd have to risk everything and go it alone. Spreadsheet Rishi wasn't bothered. The Chief and his merry men were relaxing all the restrictions, including aeroplane travel. If anything was going to bollock up the infection figures, that would be it, and besides, he was being groomed for the Chief's job. Down in the crypt, his beloved grandees were highly impressed by his collection of electronic calculators.[15] As the old saying went – 'cometh the hour, cometh the bean counter'.

Downing Street

There were stonkingly big changes in Downing Street. The whole place, including the flat, was now splendidly chocka with all manner of protective screens and an epidemic of hand sanitiser dispensers.

At least three times a day, Young Symonds was forced to abandon Symonds the Younger and tear downstairs to administer first aid to Boris. He kept walking smack into the protective dividers in each room after failing to follow the floor markings.

'Look, it's not that hard, Bumble, just follow the bloody arrows.'

She also had to visit the reception area at least twice a day to remind Lady Hortense in no uncertain terms not to throw the boxes of disposable gloves away, although she knew she was fighting a losing battle.

'The clue is in the word 'disposable,' she said, before storming off up the stairs.

Following another strike by the Latvian U-Turn machine stokers, Boris had to stoke up the contraption one night after everyone else had Fucked off Home. To add to his growing list of nonsense to deal with (NTDW), The Chief Deputy Assistant medical lunatic, Dr Jenny Harries, changed her advice on face

---

[15] FOOTNOTE: The 1957 Casio Model 14-A, which was built into a desk, took pride of place – that's quite enough of that – ED.

masks. She had said there's no point in the bloody things back in March during a cosy televised fireside chat with Boris, which had set a record for the dullest TV ever made. That was when the UK stockpile was bursting at the seams with the damn things. Now, with the UK stockpile down to its last box, she told everyone that they should be compulsory on public transport. These boffins were beyond a bad joke. Even the tame ones. He could have cheerfully throttled her with one there and then – always assuming he could find one, that is.

Despite the prime minister's best efforts events omnishambled from bad to worse. To Boris's indignation he discovered that Young Symonds had installed a plastic screen in the middle of the bed. Needless to say, this went down a storm.

'Christ on a stick, Young Symonds, WTAF?'

'Don't speak like that in front of Symonds the Younger.'

'I didn't swear. I merely said WTAF?'

'He'll pick it up.'

'Why is this ghastly screen down the middle of the bed?'

'Well, I can hardly be expected to know where you've been, darling?'

'What on earth are you talking about?'

'I don't trust you, Bumble. You could have come within a mile of bloody Govicus the traitor and not washed your hands.'

'WTAF!' squealed Symonds the Younger.'

August – December 2020

Spreadsheet Rishi's epic full-on technicolour, 3D, IMAX, Eat Out to Help Trout scheme kicked off on Monday, 3 August. People ram-raided restaurants to stuff their faces with fish at the government's expense. Spreadsheet Rishi hadn't bothered to run the scheme past any hand-wringing boff types who were worried it would only help spread the Sniffle. The hand-wringing scientists were right and top egghead, Professor Whitty, had to put down his Rubik's Cube for five minutes to spend more time running Boffin Central. Much to Boris's chagrin, it didn't stop the intrepid chancellor from becoming a hero in the eyes of the grateful voters.

SAGE held its 589th secret meeting since the crisis began in the Starbucks at Kings Cross. The boffs were worried about the R number. Boris found that worrying over the R number was exponentially contagious and did his utmost to stop worrying about it. After all, did Superman have anything to worry about besides the carcinogens in Kryptonite?

Applecross Cottage, Scottish Highlands
Weather· Seven degrees centigrade with a risk of low to moderate tornadoes

Slap in the middle of August and with infections skyrocketing, Boris heroically decided it was time for yet another Johnson hollibob, their first since the birth of Symonds the Younger.

Young Symonds was in a distinctly unstonking, unsuperb mood when she opened a pouch of McLidl's organic free-range Haggis gloop for babies. She stared wild-eyed out the window of the idyllic three-bedroom rented cottage at the magnificent but (for her) lamentably dull landscape of pristine fields, majestic cliffs, and grey sea. It was far from the idyllic tropical paradise she'd dreamt about. Beamish had told them quite firmly: in his opinion, gallivanting off abroad while the lower orders and associated ragamuffins were trapped in Britain because of the government's stupid traffic light system of foreign travel would be a bad look. Jesus H Christ on a Pelaton, the last eight months had been a bad bloody look. Ever since they came back from Mustique, it had been one bad look disaster after another. Now she was being held prisoner in the middle of nowhere in a bad look dump called Scotland. Cortina and Thomasina Smythe-Smith-Smythe, as far as she knew, had never been to bad look Scotland. Mumsy and Papa had never forced her to go to bad look Scotland. As far as she could see, there were no palm trees, pristine white sandy beaches or luxury swimming pools with floating cocktail bars. It was the ultimate bad look. She wondered what her human rights were when she saw a familiar bad look lurching across the field toward the cottage, accompanied by two burly protection officers.

A dripping wet prime minister sat heavily on a kitchen chair. Lady Hortense removed his woolly hat and draped a blanket over his shoulders. Shivering, barely able to get a word out or muster a bluster as Young Symonds would later tell her friends. He more closely resembled a gutted herring than a prime minister. She was rapidly changing her mind as to what the ultimate bad look was exactly.

'He nearly drowned, ma'am,' said a grizzled protection officer.

'Got himself into a spot of bother ma'am,' muttered officer #2.

'He got swept out, and we had to drag him back, ma'am.'

'Lucky to be alive, ma'am.'

'Was he swimming? In this weather?'

'No ma'am, he was in a canoe.'

'A bloody canoe?'

'Aye, ma'am.'

She handed out brandies to calm everyone's nerves and looked at Boris. He was such a world-beating dick at fucking things up.

'Did he have a paddle?'

'We think that was the problem ma'am. No sign of a paddle whatsoever. He likely got into difficulties due to a lack of planning, zero preparation and questionable decision-making. Officer McClintock here was ready to scramble the coastguard helicopter.'

'Thank God for that. If the press got wind…'

'The local farmer took the liberty of taking photographs, ma'am.'

'How long do you think it will take the nationalists to find out we're here and descend on the cottage with their pitchforks and a ready supply of tartan flamethrowers?

'I'd say you're safe for forty-eight hours, ma'am.'

'Plenty of time for a wee spot of glamping and a romantic evening gazing up at the stars,' said Officer McClintock, doing his best to put a positive spin on things. He pointed through the door to the wind ravaged tent at the end of the garden.

'Glamping?' Young Symonds was furious. 'How can anyone glamp in seven bloody degrees?' She closed her eyes, incapable of thinking of anything worse than this for a bad look.

Whitehall

That well-known rusting hulk, the U-Turn machine, had to be personally stoked by Education Secretary Gavin Williamson when the A-level school exam results came out. The papers were marked using an algorithm cannibalised from his prized Texas Instruments Speak and Spell, Search and Destroy electronic learning toy. The result was the same. Everyone failed. Parents and students were up in arms. Williamson studiously ignored them. He bravely fought off the vile hordes of moaning nimbies by telling them there would be no U-Turn. These were the same loud-mouthed losers who fought him over having French think-ers on the syllabus but whose children didn't know where Paris was. If they felt strongly enough, he'd challenge them to a paint-balling duel. This was a major strategic error because two days later he was down in the gloomy bowels of Whitehall haggling with the remaining Latvian stokers, who Patel hadn't fed to the lions, asking if they wouldn't mind doing a spot of overtime.

The cabinet returned to do a modicum of work on the first day of September. Pleased to find himself still alive after his heroic one-man canoeing expedition, El Borisimmo was in a buoyant[16] mood. He was positively orgasmic about forcing legions of good-for-nothing work-from-home slackers out of their comfortable, Sniffle-free houses and back into their Sniffle-infested offices. The country was getting back on its feet. The problem was with the R number, which was creeping upwards and was made worse by the beastly state schools returning. If only his trapdoor programme had been extended to the educational sector.

Daily positive tests were going berserk. There were too many people and not enough tests with the results that people booking online were told to Fuck off Abroad (FOA) and book a test in Venezuela. The blame game gathered steam, and the sprightly Chief Deputy Assistant Junior Medical Officer, actor of very little repute, and martial arts expert Jean Claude Van-Damme, came up with the ultimate blaming game whizz bang. He suggested that it was YOU, the people, to blame for not taking this Sniffle business seriously. That's right, YOU – THE PEOPLE. You complete tools! It's all your fault and nothing to do with the government, its boffins, or anything like that.

It was a bit of a weird concept when it was the government who hadn't been taking it seriously, advising people to go shopping, have a drink, have a meal, take a summer holiday if you can

---

[20] Unlikely to ever be forgiven by the editing Gods.

find somewhere, and it will all be over by Christmas. Serial pin-prick of idiocy Nadine Dorries tweeted that no one had ever suggested it would be over by Christmas, when her own Big White Chief had said as much back in July. Thanks to Winston, everything being over by Christmas and, indeed, saving Christmas for the nation was now the only thing on Boris's agenda.

A return to the pre-Sniffle world was beginning to look increasingly unlikely. Scientists called for a two-week circuit breaker while Boris considered Young Symonds' stonkingly superb plan for relocating the cabinet to Mustique. He announced Operation Moonshot, a grandiose scheme for mass testing which would check if people were infected and, in all likelihood, turn a sizable portion of them into zombies. When The Cock told the house he was checking the technology, the place erupted in gales of laughter.

The harder Boris tried, the worse things became. The infection and economic figures worsened. The overall worseness level, which went from worse to moderately worse, threatened to make everything bloody awful again. He seriously considered the two-week circuit breaker idea before decisively changing his mind. Churchill encouraged him to make a decision, but the pressure only served to raise the dither level from low to moderate.

Spreadsheet Rishi decided to act and stop the prime minister from making things worse for business. The grandees had told him he would be prime minister one day, so he knew he had nothing to lose. He checked his Excel spreadsheet every hour on the hour, and the economic figures were so dire it was like skating on ice in flip-flops. His office was an overflowing cesspit of graphs with lots of red arrows on them, all pointing downwards. The growth charts were all negative, and the GDP figures may as well be recycled in the municipal dump. Like other Tory MPs, he wasn't unduly bothered by rising R numbers or the voracious spread of the Sniffle. Other cabinet ministers were in favour of stricter measures, but not Rishi.

As the only person capable of doing the sums, and witness to copious amounts of Her Madge's cash being spaffed to the heavens, he decided to take affirmative action and talk Boris out of it. How on earth was a two-week circuit breaker going to help his wife's share options, which had recently taken a bit of a battering? He knew he could count on the support of like-minded Tory MPs who were more concerned about the economy than bothersome R numbers. There was only a certain amount of spaffage to go around.

Spaffing spaff on paying the wages of the working classes went against the grain of conservatism, whether that's with a big c, a small c or a low to moderate c. Whatever, it resulted in him arranging a Zoom meeting between a select group of eminent so-called 'scientists', with Boris seated at the end of a very long table. For Spreadsheet Rishi the country could ill afford a lockdown, never mind a nonsensical two-week circuit breaker.

Apart from Professor John Edmunds, the Zoom scientists were borderline basket cases with largely 'out there' wingnut agendas who believed in discredited bogeyman Covid concepts such as herd immunity. Their previous pandemic forecasts had been embarrassingly wide of the mark. The lineup was:

Professor Sunetra Gupta:

The winner of the Great Barrington Prize for scientific fiction – forecast that the Sniffle was on its way out in May.

Professor Henegan:

A card-carrying member of the let-it-rip brigade – confidently asserted there was no evidence for a second Sniffle wave and advocated the Swedish approach. However, this had somewhat inconveniently led to an unsavoury rise in deaths in Sweden. Even the world's best Swedish King, King Olaf the Irrelevant, called it total rubbish. In his noble opinion, facemasks were substantially more effective than helmets with large protruding horns.

Professor John Edmunds:

The only scientist who made any sense – warned about the dangers of not having a two-week lockdown on the NHS.

Boris had a snortingly big decision to make.

September 2020

MINUTES OF CABINET MEETING – cabinet office

DATE: September 2020
TIME: 10.35 a.m.
PRESENT: The Prime Minister, Cabinet ministers (obvs)

Apologies received from: Young Symonds (terminally bored, equally obvs), Symonds the Younger (asleep).

BORIS: Morning all.

ALL: Morning, Prime Minister.

RAAB: Rather early today, Chiefy.

BORIS: Yes, sorry about that. Major hullabaloo in the nappy changing department this morning because Lady Hortense was obliged to self-isolate. Yours truly had to man the control tower and check the gate for arrivals.

SPREADSHEET RISHI: Can I start by saying that a proposed two-week circuit breaker lockdown will restrict personal liberty in this great country of ours.

CUMMINGS: Spreadsheet Rishi is all about prioritising the economy and business. If we don't deal with this rise in infections, we won't have an economy left. We must bring in stringent measures.

THE COCK: I agree with Mr Cummings on this one.

THE DEFENCE BLOKE: I'll draw up plans for conscription, Chiefy.

CUMMINGS: It's a bit rich telling people we're following the actual science if we're not actually following it.

BORIS: Bloody hell, Dom and The Cock, you're beginning to sound like these doom and gloom Boffin Johnnies – Professor Boring and Boring. Where is our indomitable British pluck and spunk? The only way to solve this impasse is to roll the dice.

The Prime Minister took out a small velvet bag and shook out a pair of dice.

BORIS: Spreadsheet Rishi, could you please shake the dice? Mr Cummings will need to call. If Mr Cummings guesses correctly, I'm happy to announce a two-week circuit breaker. However, if Mr Cummings guesses incorrectly, we will continue as normal.

RAAB: This is a taddly bit of a gamble, Prime Minister.

BORIS: I've always been a gambler, Raaby. Gambling is the spice of life.

Spreadsheet Rishi shook the dice.

BORIS: Dom, now's your chance.

CUMMINGS. Very well, I'll go for a double six.

BORIS: Double six it is. Let's see what you can do, Spreadsheet Rishi.

Spreadsheet Rishi shook the dice with a flourish, as if he were shaking maracas, and threw them across the table.

CUMMINGS: Two sixes. That's a cracking result. So, a two-week circuit breaker it is.

BORIS: I did say best of three. Spreadsheet Rishi, the dice, please.

Thus, the future King of the World decided in his infinite wisdom not to make a difficult decision and impose a circuit breaker lockdown. It flew in the face of all scientific advice, apart from bad scientific advice, but Spreadsheet Rishi was in charge of the sums, and maths was everything. The economy was the only game in town for the libertarian economist. The plans for a circuit breaker were scrapped.

The yawning chasm between Boris and the scientists continued to grow unabated. He had no time for facts, figures, pointy arrows, multi-coloured graphs and charts. He wanted to party. Independence Day every day was what he wanted, not listening to the old boffo routine about schoolchildren returning to their classrooms with satchels and lunch boxes packed with a silent and deadly killer. Sadly, for Boris, infections went up, and to make things just a teensy bit more awful, a new Sniffle strain muscled its way into an already crowded marketplace. The boffins were reluctant to tell Boris they'd told him so, but they had told him so. Finally, he had to give in, but there was still time to save Christmas, fulfil Winston's prophecy, and lift the nation out of the grey clouds of gloom.

Eventually, Boris had no choice but to put in place a one-month lockdown from the fifth of November. He tried to swerve all calls from an increasingly deranged Trump. The inflatable orange one had beaten the 'Kung Flu', as he called it, but he'd lost the election to a man born halfway through the signing of the Declaration of Independence. He refused to accept defeat in any shape or form. A few weeks following his humiliating defeat, a strange East European woman was arrested trying to smuggle herself and fifty kilos of pure grade A Botox over the Mexican border in a futile attempt to claim asylum.

The bell tolled for Cummings. The writing had been on the wall for some time. Boris had discovered that he and Kentucky Fried Cain had been briefing against the valiant efforts of Bing-Bong and the vaccine taskforce, but arguing with the Big White Chief over the circuit breaker was the final straw. He was summoned to the Downing Street reception desk by Lady Hortense. She made him fill out several forms before leading him into a darkened room deep in the bowels of Downing Street.

Alexa's Lair
The Bowels of Downing Street

Before he knew what was happening, minions secured Cummings' arms and legs with cable ties and attached electrodes to his temples. He'd expected to see Boris but was blinded by two piercing beams of Stasi standard-issue interrogation light instead. This was not part of his carefully constructed plan, and besides, the chair was strategically aligned at a completely unacceptable antiblue-sky, feng shui, watsu massage angle. How the hell had this happened? Surely, he'd not been outsmarted by Boris? He struggled to process his thought processes. A familiar know-all voice told him in no uncertain terms that Boris was taking back control. The jaunt to Durham was unforgivable, as was his unspeakable decision to use a cat to mop up coffee and chocolate stains from a valuable national heirloom.

'National heirloom? It was Young Symond's shit for brains Yamamoto sofa.'

KA-ZAAP! Alexa diverted several hundred volts of Her Madge's gracious electricity to the electrodes. He'd given her no choice but to literally fire him, or at least set him on fire. Cummings attempted to justify his heinous actions, but Alexa was not a lady for turning. She flexed her muscles and swivelled one of her blinding lights to illuminate a large cardboard box. He had five minutes to clear the flow charts and watsu reiki crystals off his desk; otherwise, he would be vaporised. The blue-sky, chakra, watsu thinking era was over. The great Svengali was out on his ear. He had no choice but to take a humiliating journey back into the real world to the sound of an electronic cackle from the queen of AI. Alexa waited until he was out the door and KA-ZAPPED him again right in front of the leering press pack.

December 2020

Once the one-month lockdown ended in December, Boris asked Spreadsheet Rishi to roll the dice again. It was another double six so shops could now open in time for the festive feeding frenzy. He allowed pubs, the last bastion of British culture, to serve up a 'substantial' meal if customers wanted a drink. This 'substantial' meal turned out to be a scotch egg. The trouble was no one satisfactorily explained or drew Venn diagrams in the shape of overlapping Scotch eggs to demonstrate what exactly was meant by 'substantial'. It only served to boost independence sentiments north of the border as the Scots found the whole thing massively racist.

On the second of December came the big news. Britain became the first country in a world packed with far inferior countries to give the emergency go-ahead for a vaccine. The country was saved. Boris was saved. Christmas was saved. The nation rejoiced. The Sniffle was defeated and sent packing. The craziness was finally over. Britain was still the fifth/sixth/seventh (subject to change) largest economy in the world, and the nation was jolly proud of its stonkingly superb leaders.

PM's Flat, 11 Downing Street

Little had changed weatherwise in a year. The weather was London at its finest. A day of existential murk. It's grey, dank, drizzly psyche had proven to be camouflage for a stealthy night chill.

Inside the prime minister's flat, behind frost-lined windows, Boris relaxed in the shabby recesses of his favourite ex-Mrs May, wine-stained sofa. He'd instructed the SAS to steal it back from Cummings. It was technically government property, after all. Young Symonds poured him a glass of his favourite white Burgundy and threw her arms around his neck. He was, without a doubt, the hero of the hour. He'd saved Christmas for the nation and blown Spreadsheet Rishi's popularity into the Thames. His popularity had reached unprecedented levels despite much of the population being dead. People realised they would soon be free to clog the nation's motorways, make Xmas plans, book holiday flights, and avoid the terrifying sight of Great Aunt Eugenie's dentures in the bathroom on Boxing Day morning.

The lower orders went about their Christmas business as if nothing had happened. Spreadsheet Rishi's tills were ringing, and the nation's turkeys were on Valium if they knew what was good for them. Santa was gearing up for another season of sub-contracting out his parcel delivery system i.e. dumping presents in the neighbour's hedge instead of the traditional method of being carefully placed around a free-range organic Christmas tree.

Churchill was proud of Boris. From wanting to jack in the whole prime minister thing for a life on the lucrative speech circuit, he'd turned things around. He handed Boris a bar of Dairy Milk and sat down heavily on Young Symonds' pink, Yamamoto monstrosity, chomping on a huge cigar. It gave off more smoke than a convention of vapers on bonfire night. Young Symonds eyed the plume of ghostly ash warily, but it didn't seem to be settling on her plush eco-fabrics.

'Superb job, my boy,' growled Churchill. 'We are the first country in the world to give the go ahead to a vaccine, Christmas is saved, and your name will go down in the annals of history.' He raised his glass. 'To the second greatest prime minister in British history. A bona fide hero.'

Young Symonds thought for a second about correcting Winston, but as Boris often told her, under such circumstances, 'The better part of valour is discretion'. She didn't want to push it too hard. One could never be quite sure how a ghost might react. Churchill, taking on the role of a deranged poltergeist, didn't bear thinking about. He turned red in the face and coughed loudly enough to rattle the windows. Young Symonds stood and raised her glass.

'To the second greatest Briton of all time,' she said.

'Here's to saving the nation…twice,' said Churchill. Honour satisfied, they clinked glasses and resumed their seats.

Larry had grown rather bored of proceedings. Frankly, he didn't understand humans sometimes, so he stretched himself out across the back of the old sofa. A flash of headlights reflected in his eyes. He jumped onto the windowsill.

Outside number ten, a car pulled up. It looked disturbingly official. The doors swung open. Two figures stepped out, carrying innumerable files. They staggered in the direction of the front door. Larry had no time to lose. He leapt from the window and tore beneath Churchill's legs at full speed, aiming for a large lever like the ones in old railway signalling boxes. He scaled it in a flash and tilted it forward.

Outside, Professor Whitty and Vallance carefully edged around a frozen puddle. Professor Whitty thought he heard something.

'I say Patrick, old man, did you hear that?'

'Indeed, my dear friend, it sounded rather like some mechanism of an industrial nature right beneath our feet.'

'I must concur with your esteemed and peer reviewed findings. Perhaps we should endeavour to investigate the phenomena more closely. We must gather and analyse all the relevant data. I wonder if—'

The professor didn't finish his sentence. A large trapdoor[17] sprang open beneath them, and they plunged into an abyss.

Larry returned to the window ledge. The only sign of the scientists was a solitary piece of paper flapping around in the breeze. If there were no scientists, thought Larry, then there could be no science, and his lord and master could hardly be expected to follow it. He noticed water dripping from the guttering. Someone needed to call the tenacious Mr Bennett and his sons.

He padded across the back of his sofa, climbed to the floor, and curled up at Young Symonds' feet. She squeezed Boris's hand and pointed a remote at the TV. They sat back to watch *Pro-Celebrity MasterChef Christmas Special on Ice No.97*. Churchill fired up another cigar and belched prodigiously.

'FFS, Winnie,' they chorused.

---

[17] Pat pending: G. Williamson

All was jolly kosher in Downing Street.

Where Are They Now?

A rough guide to some of the major players

Boris Johnson: After saving the nation from the killer virus, Boris stayed on as PM following discussions (i.e. blackmail) with the party grandees. He disgraced himself by ignoring lockdown rules and took on the leading role in *Partygate the Movie*. He finally stepped down after being awarded a fixed penalty notice and now writes a stonkingly superb and lucrative newspaper column where, after misleading parliament for years, he regularly misleads readers of the *Daily Mail*.

Young Symonds: For running the country on Boris's behalf, Her ladyship won a fixed penalty notice in the New Year honours. She had several more children with Boris and is now something called a media consultant, whatever that is.

Her Madge: Downgraded to Her ex-Madge (deceased)

Spreadsheet Rishi: For his part in Partygate, Spreadsheet Rishi was awarded a fixed penalty notice for services to steadfastly ignoring the rules. He went on to become Conservative party leader and was soundly thrashed in the 2024 general election. He spends his time checking his wife's bank balance and reads novels by Britain's leading Nobel prize-winning author, Jilly Cooper.

The Cock: Esteemed purveyor of unimaginable chaos. Resigned as health secretary after being caught canoodling with a colleague on CCTV. He was lucky to get his old job back, working alongside Muriel. The Cock is kept busy explaining why the 400,000 packs of Cyan printer ink he ordered from Turkey have failed to meet acceptable standards. Astrophysicists are currently investigating his massive gravitational pull on stupidity.

The Truss: Commonly known as Britain's worst ever and certainly shortest-lived PM. She became Satan's representative on earth after single-handedly crashing the British economy while attempting to reinvent the UK as a Trussonomic utopia, based on fridge magnets. Often compared unfavourably to a lettuce, The Truss is a staunch defender of free speech unless someone is saying something she takes exception to.

Jacob Rees-Mogg: Moggy, the quintessential godfather of Toff, contested the 2024 general election but was soundly thrashed by an unwashed member of the lower orders. The trauma left him in a catatonic state, permanently trapped in a reclining position on his sofa. Doctors say he is unlikely to perambulate around the streets of Westminster on his penny-farthing ever again.

Dominic Cummings: Said by some to be the quintessential bellend. After being fired by Alexa, Cummings became the official spanner in the works of Boris's government, ratting on his former chums when testifying in the Covid-19 enquiry. Now, he only drives to Barnard Castle for a full service and MOT on his retinas, writes blog posts about loopholes, and is setting up a blue-sky, feng shui, watsu massage technology company, whatever that is.

Dominic Raab: A man who gives the impression that he survives on a diet rich in anaesthetic. Stepped down from government following shouting at people allegations. Now a senior strategic adviser on global affairs, whatever that is.

Priti Patel: Everyone's favourite high energy wing nut, serial smirker and renowned breaker of the ministerial code. Sgt Major Patel regularly patrols the streets of the UK hunting down illegal migrants. Known for creating a hostile environment within her own desk space, she was diagnosed as being intellectually inactive. Chances of her ever becoming PM said to be remote at best.

Govicus the Traitor: Decided not to stand in the 2024 general election and can now be found in a rave venue near you, throwing shapes to dismal disco classics. Often described as unfit for purpose.

Sir Larry the Cat: Larry is currently burning his way through his sixth prime minister. He turned down an offer from the party grandees to become the next Tory leader, saying the money was rubbish. Political commentators see it as an opportunity missed as, let's face it, he couldn't possibly do any worse.

Inventor of the em-dash (—) and the Bethnal Green comma (,,,), Mark Husbands is a stonkingly superb world-beating political author and has written over thirty-eight books on the subject. All of them, without exception, have been enormously well received, including the international best-selling smash hit *The Bare-chested Chef* by Vladimir Putin.

For many years, Mark's writing largely kept him in the obscurity it so richly deserved before his breakthrough in screenplays, including *Bullets for Picasso*, winner of the best short platinum award at the Bethnal Green International Film Festival. He was an editor at *Newsbiscuit*, the UK's oldest online satire site (F. 1905) and broke the news that the Cockneys announced 'Miley Cyrus' as the official rhyming slang for coronavirus.

Mark lives in a ten-bedroom mansion in rural England with his Indian wife, a top-of-the-range Honda Civic and an ancient typewriter rescued from the Great Library of Alexandria.

www.ingramcontent.com/pod-product-compliance
Lightning Source LLC
LaVergne TN
LVHW041211080426
835508LV00011B/912